Captive
in the Wild

Robert V. McCarthy

The true story of a western Pennsylvania pioneer woman who was
taken prisoner by the Indians and led into captivity.

i

Address all inquiries to:

Robert V. McCarthy
2364 Collins Road
Pittsburgh, PA 15235

Front cover by Shirley A. McCarthy

Printed in the United States of America by Geyer Printing Co. Inc., of Pittsburgh, PA

Captive in the Wild

To my dearest Shirley,
Danny, Laura and Tara,
who are a part of me forever

FOREWORD

This narrative is based on the personal diary of a western Pennsylvania frontier woman, Massy Harbison. She was taken prisoner in her home during a 1792 Indian raid and with two of her children was led into the wilderness as a captive for several days.

Carrying a year old infant in her arms and six months pregnant with another child, she endured physical abuse, malnutrition, and days of exposure to rain and cold in a bitter struggle to survive, as well as great emotional distress after witnessing the murder of two sons.

While her Indian captors were the ones who committed these vicious acts, the reader should be aware the Indians claim they also were the victims of the white man's barbarity during these Indian wars two centuries ago. They claim the American forces were equally bloodthirsty, beginning with attacks on Indian tribes allied with Great Britain during the Revolutionary War and continuing well into the next century until the final massacre of the Sioux Indians at Wounded Knee in 1890. Indian villages were burned and the occupants, often women and children, were slaughtered or taken captive during this century of violence.

This narrative makes no judgment about those events or the individuals involved. It speaks only to the courage and grit of one woman during this ordeal in late May 1792. No woman in American history is more entitled to be called a heroine.

The gracious assistance of the Western Pennsylvania Historical Society, Carnegie Library of Pittsburgh and the University of Pittsburgh's Hillman Library is acknowledged. Without their generous cooperation this narrative could not have been written.

PROLOGUE

The peace that came to the new American nation with the surrender of the British forces under General Cornwallis at Yorktown to General George Washington on October 19, 1781, was not shared along the western frontier.

Several Indian tribes who had been allied with Great Britain continued to raid and pillage the frontier settlements, including the western Pennsylvania communities in the vicinity of Pittsburgh.

Between 1783 and 1790 in western Pennsylvania the Indians killed, wounded or captured approximately 1,500 men, women and children, particularly along the south side of the Ohio River just west of Pittsburgh. The raiders also took with them considerable livestock and any valuables they could carry. What they couldn't steal they slew and homes of the settlers generally were left in flames.

His patience exhausted waiting for the peace treaties with the Indians to be honored, Secretary of War Henry Knox in 1791 ordered General Arthur St. Clair to mount a military expedition against the Indian Confederacy, whose tribes had been raiding Pennsylvania and Kentucky settlements.

On October 6 of that year St. Clair's military force of 2,000 men, plus a militia contingent of 300 including some western Pennsylvania units left Fort Washington (now the City of Cincinnati) and marched north in the direction of the Miami Indian tribe villages.

General St. Clair had high expectations based partly on a successful raid by the Kentucky militia in August against the Miami village of L'Anguille in the Wabash region. The Kentucky militia was under the command of Lt. Colonel James Wilkinson, who gave General St. Clair exaggerated reports of the raid's success.

The Wilkinson raid apparently caught the Miami Indian tribes unaware, for many of the warriors were attending peace negotiations at the Dorchester Conference in Quebec under British auspices. Not only were the tribes incensed that the raid occurred while they were away in peace negotiations, but the raid also served to alert them to other possible military actions against their villages. It was a warning that would serve them well.

This was the angry state of mind of the enemy that the St. Clair's forces were going up against when they began their march. Further complicating the mission of the St. Clair forces was an October gathering of the federated tribes at Grand Rapids to hear a report on the Dorchester Conference. This resulted in a greater concentration of Indians in Ohio than St. Clair expected. And it was the beginning of a series of miscalculations and misfortunes that was to plague the American force throughout the expedition.

When St. Clair's army reached the Great Miami River it had to bivouac and wait for supplies from Fort Washington. The general also was waiting for an additional 300-man militia contingent, which was late in arriving. While waiting, the men were put to work constructing Fort Hamilton, and others began the laborious task of cutting roads through the forest and underbrush.

The road construction was under the command of General Richard Butler. He not only had to build a 12-foot-wide access through the forest to accommodate the movement of artillery, but also was required to establish a parallel road between 200 and 300 yards away as part of the St. Clair strategy.

The poor supply of axes, the blades of which were soon dulled against the trees being felled, further complicated the army's effort to clear these paths. So an exasperated General Butler finally abandoned the St. Clair strategy and ordered the men to concentrate on building a single road.

The force, weary from its construction labors and inadequate rations, also had to endure inclement weather when an early winter set in during late October. Tired from their labors and inadequately fed, the St. Clair army was in a struggle for survival in wintry weather without the proper gear.

When the march finally resumed, the same problems of scarce supplies and inclement weather prevailed. The army also had lost several horses, which either had wandered off or were stolen. All of these difficulties gave rise to bickering among St. Clair's officers and the inevitable desertion by some of the troops. General St. Clair had to order another halt in mid-October in an area that was about five miles south of what is today the Ohio community of Greenville. While awaiting the delivery of more late supplies he ordered the construction of another fortification, Fort Jefferson.

Before the army could again resume its march north, General St. Clair suffered an attack of rheumatic asthma and gout in his left arm. He insisted that the force keep moving north in spite of his ailments. By now, however, the Miami Indians and their allies had become aware of the approaching force and were preparing to meet it.

General St. Clair was cheered by the arrival of the Americans' Indian ally, Chief Piamingo of the Chickasaw Tribe, in early November when the march resumed. But his presence proved to be of small consequence in the ensuing battle. The night before the planned attack on the main Miami Indian village the force bivouacked a few miles away on the St. Mary River. This waterway led to the St. Joseph River where the main Miami village, Kekionga, was located (near what is now Fort Wayne).

Unfortunately for St. Clair's army, however, on October 28 a force of more than 1,000 Indians had departed the Miami village and headed in St. Clair's direction. They were led by renowned Miami War Chief Me-she-kin-no-quah (Little Turtle) and Blue Jacket of the Shawnees. The force also included warriors from the Wyandots, Delawares, Ottawas, Chippewas and Potawtons (all tribal members of the Indian Confederation).

When his army established its camp the night before it was to attack the Miami village, General St. Clair ordered the 300-man militia to camp on the other side of the river, leaving the waterway as a divider between his troops.

While the deployment was in progress some Indians were seen observing the troops and then they quickly departed. For some unknown reason General St. Clair was not alarmed at the Indians' presence and he apparently discounted the possibility that they would have sufficient time to alert the enemy.

It was his intention to build a stockade at this location the following morning where the men could leave their packs and any other personal belongings that were not necessary for the coming battle. He also intended to leave behind in the stockade the wives and children some of the troops had foolishly brought along with them as camp followers. It was a shelter the general and his troops would never build.

Shortly before sunrise the following morning the Miami warriors had surrounded the St. Clair forces and opened fire on the militia's forward position. In fear of being overrun by a far superior force, this inadequately trained force abandoned its position and fell back to the main camp. Their unexpected arrival created disorder and confusion within the ranks of the army regulars, and soon near total chaos prevailed.

A volley of rifle fire deterred the attacking Indian force temporarily, but soon the natives resumed the assault and concentrated their efforts against the center of the defense perimeter where the artillery was located.

Seeing the confusion and heavy casualties that resulted from the attack, Lt. Colonel Drake led a bayonet charge that turned the Indians' left flank and drove them back for several hundred yards. The advantage was lost, however, for want of a sufficient number of riflemen to pursue the retreating force. The Miami tribe returned to the attack and was again repulsed by a bayonet charge, but each engagement took a heavy toll in the number of wounded and dead.

With the artillery overrun and most of his officers already dead, St. Clair faced a critical void in leadership for the outmaneuvered and inexperienced American troops in his command. Retreat was his only option. He was stunned, however, when in the process of falling back his troops abandoned most of their supplies and weapons, including their artillery.

Several of the wounded also were abandoned and many a surviving soldier carried with him the terrifying memory of comrades, some still alive, being tomahawked and scalped. Included among the casualties were many of the women and children who had accompanied the troops. They also were caught in the trap and suffered the same fate.

Remnants of the retreating army finally reached the road that led away from the battle scene and there the St. Clair army completely lost its poise. In fleeing the massacre the undisciplined soldiers, much to the amazement of their officers, discarded their rifles along the way. General St. Clair would later report to Secretary Knox with great disgust that the retreat route back to Fort Jefferson was strewn with these weapons that he could not retrieve because his army had lost all of its horses.

In all probability there would have been even fewer survivors, but the fleeing soldiers were aided in their escape by the uncontrolled greed of their pursuers. The Indians broke off the attack because they wanted to return to the abandoned camp and share in the loot that had been left behind by St. Clair's troops.

The retreat to Fort Jefferson covered a distance of 29 miles, so the surviving defeated force didn't arrive at the fort until shortly after sunset. In the battle's wake were 593 killed or missing and

214 wounded who managed to escape.

News of St. Clair's defeat spread rapidly through the western Pennsylvania settlements. It gave rise to immediate fears of bolder Indian attacks to come, for the pioneer families knew the Indians would interpret the victory over General St. Clair's army as proof that the frontier was now unprotected and ripe for pillaging and murder.

1
Apprehension

The morning of May 22, 1792, had just arrived. As the early morning light leaked through the cracks of the cabin door it was apparent that the coming day was going to be clear and warm, reassuring the sleepy-eyed Massy Harbison of the beautiful days of late spring and summer that were just ahead. Massy had intended to rise when the two lodgers (men who served with her husband, John, as spies in the army under General Arthur St. Clair) left the cabin. With her 12-month-old infant, John, awake in her arms and nursing at her breast, however, she decided to remain within the protective warmth of her bed and wait for the child to slumber once again.

Five-year-old son Robert and three-year-old Samuel also were asleep. When the infant had his fill he too dozed off and Massy soon joined them in the serenity of this late May morning slumber.

Peaceful repose at daybreak or any other time in the pioneer settlements near Pittsburgh had suddenly become a rarity. For now there was the new and frightening reality of Indian attacks in their Allegheny River community (about 22 miles east of Pittsburgh) and throughout western Pennsylvania where heretofore these incidents had been confined to settlements to the west of Pittsburgh along the Ohio River.

Indeed, fear of Indian raids for the past year had completely changed what once was a joyous and promising existence for John and Massy Harbison. It had compelled them for the sake of safety to abandon their previous isolated homestead near the headwaters of Chartiers Creek. They had enjoyed a very prosperous two years from 1789 to 1791. Now they were settled in a new cabin where life wasn't as prosperous, but it was safer being in sight of a blockhouse built in response to the Indian raids.

Married in 1787 at the age of 17 over her father's objections, Massy's married life had its negative side from the very beginning. Her father, Edward White, had opposed the marriage, citing several reasons, including her young age, as justification for his negative response. But that was a superficial argument. His primary objection was John Harbison's swaggering image as a handsome, tough woodsman who found fulfillment in the dangerous atmosphere of the frontier wilderness where he had to match brain and brawn with the Indians.

"Men like John Harbison make great soldiers, and we need them," he said to his daughter. "But they make poor husbands."

Massy had great affection for her father. He had been a patriot in support of the Revolution and a devoted father. They had lived in Hamell Township, New Jersey, during the war years while her father served as a contractor with the army. He was involved in almost every major battle of the war.

As a young school girl Massy had the rare experience of observing a battle in progress. On the day of the battle of West Field she and several of her classmates left school and mounted a high plateau overlooking what they thought was the bivouac area for the American troops. When they arrived, however, they were looking down on the battlefield just as hostilities were about to begin.

It had been a little too close to reality for Massy, for she could hear the frightening, loud volleys of cannon fire and observe men falling to the ground either in pain or in total silence when hit with flesh-tearing shrapnel or bullets from unfriendly muskets.

In celebration of the American victory at the end of the war in 1783 and in anticipation of an exciting and prosperous future, Edward White moved his family to western Pennsylvania.

But four years later in 1787 Massy was in love with John Harbison and tried to convince Edward White that this handsome young woodsman was worthy of her hand. She was unsuccessful in the attempt.

Massy insisted that John was not the adventurer her father made him out to be. "He isn't like that. He has found good soil in a location near Chartiers Creek and we will farm it when we are married."

Her father knew Massy could have just about any eligible beau along the Allegheny River settlements. She was pretty, and young men enjoyed her company. He was convinced she could do much better than John Harbison.

In fact, that is what he expected to happen until the 1786 annual corn roast held by several of the pioneer families and their guests after the harvest that year. It was a popular gathering for people of all ages, but the young ladies and gentlemen especially cherished it as one of the few occasions when they could meet and get to know members of the opposite sex.

Massy was with some of the unmarried women when she and John Harbison met for the first time at this social gathering and the attraction was immediate for both of them. A trapper and hunter by trade who was usually dressed in buckskins, the six-foot-tall John Harbison wore his one and only finely tailored brown coat for this occasion. With his broad shoulders, handsome features, dark brown eyes and black hair tapering halfway down his back in a pony tail, he was easily the most impressive eligible bachelor present.

Massy was equally prominent with her slim figure neatly fitted into a white frock that featured a blue collar and blue sash. Most everyone at the affair came with great expectations of tasting one of Massy's delicious fruit pies, but the young men who came went away daydreaming about one day tasting her lips.

"They tell me you are the best baker on the frontier," said John Harbison after his introduction to Massy. It was an invitation he previously arranged with the wife of a fellow trapper.

Massy recognized the flirtation. She smiled and responded, "That is for others to say, sir. Not me."

"Come now, let me say it for you. When a beautiful lady like you is complimented about her cooking she has a right to be proud. It sort of wins the day for you, don't you think?"

Massy was enjoying the exchange, but she didn't want it to be obvious that she was impressed with this tall, sturdy, handsome frontiersman.

The inevitable courtship soon followed in spite of Edward White's misgivings. At first Massy's father expected the relationship to falter because of Harbison's frequent absences in the wilderness. But it did not. His intervention now bordered on the desperate as he tried to persuade his daughter to change her course.

"There are some very promising bachelors in these settlements who will make good providers for their families," he reminded Massy. "Some have already asked if they can court you. Why won't you at least see them?"

"I am flattered," she responded, "but, Father, I don't love any of them. I love John Harbison and I am going to marry him."

The relationship between Massy and her father was never the same after that conversation. Until then he had been barely cordial to John Harbison. After Massy's talk of marriage he refused to speak to him at all and barely spoke to his daughter.

When Massy and John were married they lived the first two years near her father's Redstone Fort home in hopes of achieving a reconciliation. Her first child, Robert, was born there and John spent those days attending to his wife and son by seeing to their needs and being there for them. But Edward White was unimpressed. Even the birth of his first grandchild failed to reconcile him. When it was finally apparent that Massy's father would not accept John Harbison as his daughter's husband, the separation became painfully permanent. John and Massy relocated and began homesteading at the Chartiers Creek location.

* * *

The peace that came to the new American nation when the Revolutionary War ended did not extend to the nation's western frontier. It surely did not exist in the western Pennsylvania area where Indian nations like the Miami and Shawnee tribes, who had been allied with the British, continued their war against the settlers.

The Indian attacks were often so fierce that even the white settlers who wanted to live in peace with the Indians were reluctant to espouse such a controversial cause. Massy had been so inclined, arguing with her husband that the Indians were not without cause for their warlike actions when white hunters and trappers continued to enter lands assigned to the Indians by treaty in total disregard of the consequences of their actions. John Harbison held to the more popular frontier view that treaties with "savages" were the worthless promises of politicians, which they never meant to keep. Indeed, the new American nation rarely demanded that its settlers comply with the treaty agreements it had made with the Indians.

The tribes were aware of this and they were angry with those chieftains who made treaties with the untrustworthy American government. In addition, bitterness still prevailed among some of the tribes over the bloody battles waged during the war, including the Continental Army's penchant for burning out the villages of hostile tribes and the often random slaying of their inhabitants, women and children included.

The Miami and Shawnee tribes also were not appeased over a peace treaty that was reached between the new United States government and the Indian Federation's representatives in 1783. For many of the tribes, therefore, Cornwallis didn't represent them when he surrendered to General Washington. Their war continued.

The first strike along the Allegheny River had occurred more than a year before this glorious May morning on March 18, 1791, at the home of Thomas Dick near the mouth of Deer Creek. Dick and his wife were taken prisoner and a young man who lived with them was killed and scalped.

Because the Dicks' home wasn't that far away, word of their capture alarmed Massy, as well as the rest of the Allegheny River frontier. But the report of an even more frightening episode was soon to follow. Four days later (on March 22) the Abraham Russ massacre took place. Eleven men, women and children (including Russ) were tomahawked to death in the Russ cabin about two miles above the mouth of Bull Creek, just 23 miles above Pittsburgh.

In what seemed like a miracle, some of the settlers who were in the Russ cabin managed to escape during the killing and the confusion. They made their way to the Allegheny River where a young courageous frontiersman came across the river in a canoe and brought them back across the waterway to safety. These settlers survived and their account of the massacre traveled swiftly by word of mouth to every frontier home in western Pennsylvania. The peaceful existence of the Allegheny River settlements had been destroyed and the settlers were filled with foreboding.

Word of the slaughter reached the Harbison household as well as several other families living along the Allegheny within hours of the incident. With her husband, John, away from home on one of his frequent excursions with the army in the wilderness, Massy immediately decided that it no longer was safe for her and the children to remain in their cabin.

"We are going for a ride tonight," she told her oldest child, Robert, "but you must promise me to keep total silence."

It sounded like some sort of game to her oldest son, the almost four-year-old Robert, and that was fine with Massy.

"I can't tell the children of the possible dangers," she told herself, and she was grateful that they were too young to question why they had to vacate their cabin so suddenly.

Young Samuel was not old enough to comprehend, but Robert was overjoyed as he anticipated the nighttime ride. Sitting on a horse on a ride through the woods at night with his mother was the most exciting adventure in his young life. Of course, he assured Massy, he would keep silent.

Massy was less than fit for travel herself, especially in the total darkness of night. In addition to the two small children to look after, she was seven months pregnant with her third child. But she knew the prudent thing to do was leave, regardless of the difficulty, for they would be helpless if the Indians came to the Harbison cabin. So Massy packed what little she could carry, mounted a horse with her younger child, Samuel, in her arms and tied Robert behind her. Then they set out for the home of James Paul (about seven miles away) in total darkness.

It was a journey that was fraught with trepidation for a young housewife and mother of two small children. She was not that familiar with the trail and was most fearful that in the dark of the forest they might stray off the trail and not realize it.

As the horse plodded along that path Massy tried to remember the twists and turns which were only vaguely familiar to her in daylight. "I could end up going in the opposite direction and not know it," she worried.

Fear of stumbling into an Indian ambush was her greatest concern and it intensified with each strange noise they heard in the forest as they rode along.

"I must not alarm the children," she kept reminding herself. "So let Robert enjoy himself as long as he is quiet."

The entire journey, of course, was totally lost on young Samuel, who fell asleep shortly after the trip began.

Massy was grateful for that and for the obedience of the silent Robert. She knew it was necessary to at least appear calm in order not to alarm her children. This meant acting brave in front of them,

6

so every time a noise from the forest sounded, she reassured Robert with a gentle hug and silently prayed that the sounds were not man-made.

"If John was only with us," Massy thought to herself, ignoring the reality of what little one man could do in the dark to protect his wife and children against hostiles. But he wasn't there and she knew she and the children were on their own until they reached safety. Her only ally was her God and she made certain He would not forget her by quietly praying to Him for deliverance throughout the night.

Massy felt a great sense of relief when shortly after the first light of dawn the Paul residence came into view. She also was grateful and relieved that so many other pioneer family neighbors had made the same journey. Close to 80 women and children, who had fled their homes in response to the news of the Indian raid on the Russ cabin, arrived at approximately the same time at the same location.

The men in the group had not remained there very long. All but four left almost immediately, intent on pursuing the raiding Indians. Massy was less than reassured at the sight of the men departing and leaving behind such a small contingent of males to defend the women and children gathered there. She hoped they wouldn't return from this masculine display of bravado in the woods to find the women and children murdered or taken captive

The men's search proved to be an unsuccessful one, but it did accomplish one thing. Before returning they selected a location for a blockhouse on the Allegheny River (about one mile below the Kiskiminetas River and erected it as security against another Indian attack. The Harbisons were grateful over the site that was selected, for it was within view of their cabin.

The men returned after a few days. In the absence of additional incidents, those who had earlier fled were sufficiently reassured and returned to their homes.

It was in response to these incidents, however, that the Secretary of War, Henry Knox, ordered General Arthur St. Clair to organize a military expedition and march against the marauding Miami tribe in western Ohio.

It was an order that caused some anxious moments in several frontier households, including the Harbison cabin, for John Harbison was among the men who joined the militia for a six-month tour of duty. Massy protested about the risk he was taking and the jeopardy his departure created for her and the children. But with his family in a cabin within sight of the blockhouse, John saw no such danger.

Massy's fears were more than justified, for in the early November conflict that followed between St. Clair's ill-prepared forces and the Indians, John Harbison was one of the casualties. But he was one of the more fortunate among the wounded in that ill-fated expedition. His wounds were not that serious, so he was able to escape with the rest of General St. Clair's retreating forces. Ultimately he returned home to Massy and the children in late December to recuperate.

Sensing that more Indian attacks were imminent, Massy again urged her husband to leave General St. Clair's service so he could be with his family in the event that the Indians raided their settlement. But John Harbison was quick to dismiss his wife's pleadings.

"How much danger can there be with the cabin so close to the blockhouse?" he asked Massy as his wounds healed and he began to anticipate returning to General St. Clair's service.

Massy reminded him, "I have two small children and we soon will have a third. How can you ignore the dangers we face and the burdens I must bear in your absence?" she asked. But within three months John's recuperation was complete and he was once again ready to return to the woods and the Indian wars.

The challenges and dangers of military expeditions attracted him and he seemed to be energized by the potential of combat with the Indians. So when the army was informed of his recovery, and in spite of Massy's protests, John returned to General St. Clair's service as a spy. Soon after on March 22, 1792, he was ordered back into the woods to keep watch on the Indians and report back on their movements.

Once more Massy was left alone to cope with the demands of raising her small children in the face of this new Indian menace. With the earlier birth of the Harbisons' third son, John, the children now numbered three. An additional complication was her fourth pregnancy. John managed to return home on occasion over the following two months, but his presence was too brief to be reassuring for his wife.

The strain also became apparent in their marriage and Massy could not help but remember the objections her father first raised to her union with John Harbison. Thoughts about her father were always painful for Massy because she still loved and respected him, but they had not been reconciled. These thoughts and the danger of the current circumstances only served to aggravate her loneliness.

* * *

Her son John suddenly stirred in Massy's arms and awakened her once more. Quiet still prevailed in the cabin, but Massy was awake now and her thoughts were of more recent events. Just a week before, her husband had returned with several of his spy comrades. They had come to the cabin after dark and John asked Massy to prepare their supper.

She was less than overjoyed over this sudden imposition. It already was late at night and she had just put her young children to bed. Massy knew that a group of Indian fighters sitting around a dinner table late at night and exchanging stories about their experiences in the frontier wars would create too much of a disturbance for the children to sleep.

Some of the spies lived near enough that they could have gone to their own homes. But they knew they would not be served as delicious a supper as Massy would eventually put before them. Her reputation as a cook was known all along the Allegheny River settlements. But men also enjoyed Massy's company because unlike many frontier housewives she still had retained her fine features in spite of giving birth to three children and now bearing a fourth.

But all of this was lost on Massy. For in addition to being imposed upon at such a late hour, she was unhappy to have to leave the security of the cabin at night to go to the spring house for food. And her husband's seeming indifference to the danger she would be exposed to didn't sit well with her. In fact, Massy had to refrain from saying anything, lest the anger in her voice be detected and make John's guests uncomfortable.

Fortunately, one of the younger men among the spies detected her concern.

"I will be happy to accompany you to the spring house, Mrs. Harbison," he assured her.

"Thank you. I would appreciate that. Perhaps you can help me carry some of the provisions," she told him.

"I most certainly will," he replied, as he lifted his musket from where he had leaned it against the wall when the men entered the cabin.

Massy didn't know if the young man was married or single, but as they walked along she again expressed her appreciation.

"It was gracious of you to offer to help," she offered in an effort to continue conversation with an adult. That was a rare opportunity for Massy these days with her husband away and her life centered around three children.

"You must be hungry after being in the woods so long and living on limited rations," Massy continued.

"I am," he answered, "particularly when I have the opportunity to satisfy my hunger at your splendid table."

"You are kind," she said, "but I am sure your wife sets a good table."

"She would if I had one," he replied with a chuckle, "but I am not married."

"What a waste," Massy thought to herself. "But someday he will make a good husband because he was such a considerate young man."

The spring house was only a short distance away. When they reached it the young man stood outside facing the surrounding forest while Massy went inside.

Within a few moments she had gathered the provisions she would need for supper and turned to walk to the spring house door. That is when Massy distinctly heard the sound that came from the woods like the bleating of a lamb or fawn. The young spy also heard it and alertly dropped to one knee and brought his rifle to the ready position.

Both of them were alarmed that the origin of the sound might be something more menacing than a tranquil animal in the dark. They stood motionless and listened in silence, but heard nothing else. Both knew that if an animal was the source of the sound they would most likely hear it again. But there was only silence now.

Gathering her supplies in her arms, Massy quickly moved to the entrance to the spring house. She and the young soldier glanced at each other and then hurried to reach the cabin.

* * *

The sound Massy and her spy escort heard was real enough, for it came from the two-legged variety of species, not a lamb or a fawn. As the spy suspected, it was a signal. It came from Alishawa of the Miami Indian tribe as he observed the activity at the spring house from nearby concealment in the woods near the Harbison cabin. His

10

signal was directed to two other tribesmen who had taken up concealed positions closer to the spring house.

The prearranged signal directed them to remain where they were until he joined them and to take no rash actions on their own initiative. It was a necessary precaution because one of those Miami tribesmen was a young and angry warrior named Maumeedoe, and Alishawa knew the sight of a helpless frontier housewife and one young escort was a temptation Maumeedoe would find overwhelming.

He quietly made his way to where he left them and indicated with a motion of his hand that they should depart. Maumeedoe scowled to let Alishawa know he disagreed.

"We can kill them now," he said in a harsh whisper, "and those inside the cabin before they know we are here."

Alishawa was irritated and made no effort to conceal his anger. "I am responsible for this scouting party," he snarled as he stepped up to his young companion, "and I say move, *NOW*."

By this time Massy and the young man had reached the cabin door. Alishawa knew that once the white people went inside they would relate what they had heard and that the woods soon would be flooded with white scouts and soldiers looking for them. Maumeedoe hadn't lost any of his anger, but he knew he couldn't win the argument, so he and the other warrior turned and stepped in the direction from which they had come earlier that day.

They had been sent to scout the blockhouse and surrounding settlements by Miami Chief Little Turtle. He wanted to know what size of force would be necessary to make a successful attack on the blockhouse and destroy it. It was a source of the white settlers' strength and the Miamis wanted the settlements along the Allegheny River to be vulnerable to their attacks.

Nothing else was said as the three Indians put distance between themselves and the cabin, but Maumeedoe still wanted to argue the point as soon as they were out of this section of the forest. They made their way to the Allegheny River bank where the bark-skin canoe they had earlier hidden in the brush was retrieved and placed in the water.

As the three plowed their oars into the water and the canoe swiftly moved away from shore, Maumeedoe took up the argument again. "We should have killed them now. You know in time one of us will have to kill all of them. Why not do it now and have that many less white soldiers to fight?"

"Maumeedoe," replied Alishawa, "you know why, or at least you should. We were directed to spy on that settlement and bring information back to Little Turtle so we can plan an assault on the fort." He continued as the three of them labored with their canoe paddles and passed the midpoint of the river. "If we killed all of them in that cabin tonight, what would we have accomplished? The blockhouse still would be there and the white soldiers would be alerted that we might attack it."

Little Turtle was a warrior of great renown among the Miami tribe's Shawnee and Delaware allies as well as his own tribe. He enjoyed the reputation as a wise warrior by planning attacks based on intelligence from his scouts. It was precisely for this reason that he directed Alishawa to lead this small scouting party to spy on the fortress and the surrounding settlements. Bringing back a few scalps from a nearby cabin and thus alerting the soldiers of the plan to attack would have displeased him greatly.

Nearing the age of 40 years, Alishawa was not reputed to be a great warrior. But he was wise as an observer when scouting the settlements. Little Turtle valued his observations and his judgment, which is why Alishawa was in charge of the scouting party.

He was of average height, less than six feet tall, but he was husky. With the right design of war paint on his face he could even look fierce to a frightened white settler. Indeed, more than once in battle his appearance had given him the upper hand when in reality his fighting skills were only average.

Not so with Maumeedoe. He stood six feet, four inches and needed no war paint to look fierce. And he was as ruthless and reckless in the attack as he looked. He had sliced away many a white scalp and was fond of doing so while his victim lay before him incapacitated but conscious.

It was Maumeedoe's habit of shouting to gain attention as he marched back into the Miami village with the scalps he had claimed held high and still dripping blood down his muscular bare arm. He was slim in stature, but his muscles tolerated no soft flesh on his limbs and torso.

His style of attack, however, was accompanied by an often irrational disregard for his safety or the safety of his companions. He often exposed himself to enemy fire unnecessarily and in doing so also risked the lives of the other warriors. In fact, one of Little Turtle's sons had been severely wounded a year earlier in the surprise attack on General Arthur St. Clair's army near the Miami village because Maumeedoe was impatient to join the battle and kill the hapless soldiers who were fleeing the battle scene. One of them hadn't been so hapless. He suddenly stopped, wheeled around and fired his musket. The bullet just missed Maumeedoe, but it ripped through the upper chest of Little Turtle's inexperienced 17-year-old son as he emerged from his well-concealed position to follow Maumeedoe.

Little Turtle was forever grateful to the English doctor in Detroit whose knowledge of medicine saved the young warrior's life. But he was forever unforgiving of Maumeedoe's irrational priority of salvaging scalps and his reckless impatience for ignoring the mission assigned him.

Alishawa was aware of Maumeedoe's weaknesses as well as his prowess as a warrior. Because the older man knew that bravery in the face of enemy fire was a quality the outmanned Miamis could not afford to overlook, he had hoped by example to convince Maumeedoe of the need to anticipate his enemy's reaction before he charged into the attack. His first impressions were that Maumeedoe would take some convincing.

Alishawa had another reason for avoiding bloodshed on this mission. He had been smitten by the comely appearance of the frontier woman who had come to the spring house. From his observations made from the woods when the three Indians arrived on their scouting mission just before dusk, he presumed that woman also was the mother of the two small boys who were playing outside the cabin door. She was a pretty rather young woman who was prolific in bearing sons, which was an asset this Indian could not overlook.

* * *

Once safely inside the cabin Massy and the young spy related to the men gathered there the noises they had heard while at the spring house. The men immediately left the cabin and conducted a search of the vicinity. When they found no evidence of unwanted intruders, however, they dismissed the incident as the harmless noise from some animal and went back to the cabin to await the late supper. But Massy was not convinced. Nor was the young frontiersman who had been with her.

Still unnerved by the experience, the next morning Massy pleaded with John to move her and the children to a more secure location. But John Harbison was convinced his family faced no real danger because of the close proximity of the blockhouse to his cabin, so he once again dismissed Massy's concerns as unwarranted.

* * *

A week had passed without further incident, so John Harbison and his fellow spies were convinced that imaginations had been working overtime for Massy and the young spy. But Massy was unconvinced and she continued to emphasize to her husband the urgency of her situation of being alone with three small children.

While she lay in her bed that late May morning drifting in and out of sleep with these troublesome thoughts ever present in her mind, she found herself hoping the two departed lodgers who had stayed overnight in the cabin had remembered to lock the cabin door when they departed.

"I will make certain," she promised herself, "when I rise."

2

The Raid

The comfort of her soft, warm bed ended abruptly for Massy. Something strong and unrelenting suddenly gripped her ankle. She was not fully awake, so she wondered if she was caught in the middle of a bad dream. Next she tried to pull her ankle free, but what gripped her would not yield. Then suddenly she felt her body being yanked from beneath the blanket and she slammed to the cabin floor.

Massy knew it was no dream.

Her bewilderment now became fright. Because she was still facing the cabin wall, she didn't know who the scoundrel was who had invaded her home.

"Who are you and how dare you force your way into my home?" she screamed as her emotions bounced back and forth between indignation and fear for herself and her children.

The infant in her arms was equally upset over the rude awakening because his body also hit the floor and he was making his protest known with loud wailing.

The infant was in the grip of her right arm, so Massy folded her left hand into a firm fist and thrust the left arm in a backhanded upward swing, hoping to catch her attacker by surprise with a blow to his face. But her arm was met by a large and powerful hand that grasped her wrist and terminated all of her resistance by painfully twisting the arm behind her back.

She turned her head to protest, then she drew back in horror because she was staring into the painted face of an angry, snarling Indian.

"What do you want?" Massy demanded.

But the Indian did not understand English, so he snarled at her in response.

Now glancing around the cabin she realized there were more than just this one intruder. Indeed, the room was full of Indians milling about and bearing muskets, knives and tomahawks.

Death for her and her children, she was certain, was only moments away.

Her sons Robert and Samuel stared unbelieving from their beds. The three-year-old seemed more confused than frightened, but fear was clearly apparent in the expression on the face of Robert.

Massy's fear also was apparent, for her body was trembling as she scrambled to her feet, still clutching the infant in her right arm. "Take what you want, but leave me and my children alone," she shouted.

The Indians were unimpressed with her bravado and ignored her. Their interest now clearly was outside of the cabin where they were looking in the direction of the blockhouse.

Massy now became aware of her scanty attire in a room full of hostile men. In an effort to better cover her body she reached out for a petticoat near her bed to add to the one flimsy petticoat she was wearing.

The Indian who had accosted her remained nearby and appeared to resent her effort to achieve modesty. He snatched the petticoat from her hands, grunted and threw the garment to the floor.

"I'm only trying to get decent," Massy protested.

The Indian, who was called Maumeedoe, neither understood what she said nor cared.

Massy reached for another garment, and yet another, but each time Maumeedoe forcefully ripped it away.

"Please, I need some clothes," she demanded.

All of the confusion was too much for the infant in her arms. Young John resumed bellowing in loud and angry screams. Massy thought his cries would surely carry all the way to the blockhouse.

Several of the Indians were standing by the beds of Robert and Samuel, and Massy was again filled with trepidation.

"Please don't hurt my children," she started to say, but the Indians ignored her. One of them lifted first Samuel and then Robert and deposited them onto the floor.

Massy was relieved that he apparently meant no harm to the children and offered a silent prayer of thanks.

Now that the children were out of their beds, the intruders grabbed the featherbeds from under the blankets, carried them to the cabin door and emptied them. Massy soon realized why. The empty bedding was to be used to carry whatever possessions they chose to remove from the cabin. Once the feathers were spilled onto the cabin floor several of the Indians started to take an interest in the Harbison possessions and quickly went about the task of tossing possessions into the featherbed bags. What they didn't think was worth keeping was tossed aside or smashed.

The pilfering of material possessions was the least of Massy's concern. "They can have it all," she told herself, "if they will only leave me and the children alone."

So Massy shouted out, "Take what you want and leave." She was surprised that her voice sounded so strong, for she had never been so frightened. But the Indians continued to ignore her.

Five-year-old Robert realized the safest place to be in the cabin was beside his mother. He began ever so slowly to ease his way over to her. Samuel, however, was more angry than scared over the intrusion. He began to walk in the direction of the fireplace where he sought the warmth of the fire that the earlier departing lodgers had thoughtfully lit. Some of the Indians appeared to be amused by the small child's seeming indifference to their presence.

Samuel settled in front of the fire and began to warm himself. But he didn't stop whimpering and this was quickly becoming quite an irritation to the Indian braves around him.

Seeing the danger Samuel might be creating for himself, Massy became alarmed. But the child was by now on the other side of the cabin and beyond her reach. So she tried to get his attention by motioning to him. But he didn't see her.

Most of the Indians in the cabin ignored these incidents. They were more concerned about what was beyond the cabin door at the blockhouse, while the others were looting valuables from the shelves along the walls of the cabin. Massy realized that Maumeedoe did neither. He kept an unnerving watch on the captives.

This war party had a single purpose in this raid. They had been ordered by Chief Little Turtle to destroy the blockhouse. That was their only goal. If they could pick up some of the white man's treasures and capture some prisoners along the way, so much the better.

This was not apparent to Massy, who kept repeating, "Take whatever you want." They still ignored her as she repeated it and added, "Leave me and my children alone."

Some of the Indians started to laugh. "You think you are in a position to bargain with us," said one in English as he smiled at her.

"I didn't know you could speak English," she replied. "What do you want with me and my children? We are no threat to you. Why harm us?"

"You will know soon enough," he replied, and he was no longer smiling. "So stand there, be silent and keep your children silent."

Robert and John were still, but Samuel continued to linger near the fireplace and whimper.

"If there is a chance for our survival," Massy told herself, "we will have to get outside of the cabin." She and Robert were near the cabin door, so they didn't have far to go. But what about Samuel?

"Samuel," she called, "please come to me."

This was breaking the silence the invaders had imposed, but Massy hoped they would understand she was trying to comply with their wishes.

The child was staring into the fire and ignoring the Indians, but he looked up when his Mother beckoned, looked in her direction, and then he turned back to the fire.

Massy saw Maumeedoe glaring at the child and his fierce expression frightened her.

She felt a little hand slide inside of hers. It was Robert's and he was trembling. With John now in her left arm, Massy went down on one knee and wrapped her right arm around her oldest son and hugged him.

The Indians continued to ignore Massy and the children, so she began to lead Robert in a slow, deliberate walk in the direction of the cabin door.

Before she reached the doorway she tried once more to attract Samuel's attention. This time, however, she motioned with her hand in the hopes that he would look up and get her message. But the child was still whimpering by the fireplace with his back to his mother, so he couldn't see Massy's hand signal for him to join them.

The thought of reaching the outside and possible escape while Samuel was still inside the cabin was painful for Massy. She did not want to abandon him to the mercy of their captors. "But I owe it to the other children to get them to safety first," she reminded herself. It was a painful dilemma for a mother to face, but Massy knew what choice she had to make.

Leaning down in Robert's direction, she whispered, "Try to get out of the cabin."

"What about Samuel?" he asked.

"I'll come back for him," Massy assured Robert, knowing in her heart, however, that it was a promise she never could keep.

Nearing the cabin door, which the Indians had left ajar, Massy glanced back one more time at Samuel, hoping he would see her signal and come to her. He still preferred the warmth of the fireplace and he still had his back to her. There was no alternative.

"Oh no," said Massy as she reached the open door and peered outside.

There were more Indians outside of the cabin, and behind the cover of the surrounding trees they were advancing in the direction of the blockhouse.

The Indians' plan was now apparent. Their mission was to attack the blockhouse. Capturing or killing Massy and her children was secondary.

"How foolish of me to think we could get away," she said to herself.

Just then one of the soldiers emerged through the blockhouse gate carrying an empty pail and was walking leisurely in the direction of the spring for water. He didn't see the ambush that was quickly taking shape and he was walking right into it. Three Indians were maneuvering to get between him and the blockhouse and would soon cut him off from his retreat path.

Massy's reaction was automatic.

"Help," she screamed, "there are Indians here!"

The startled soldier looked in Massy's direction and immediately saw the Indians and the danger confronting him.

The Indians also were startled, for they had momentarily forgotten about Massy and her children.

The startled soldier dropped the empty pail, turned back to the blockhouse and ran with all of the strength he could muster. The Indians opened fire, but they too had been unnerved by Massy's warning and the first volley of bullets missed their mark.

Another shot exploded from the rifle of one of the attackers and this time the soldier gripped his right arm and staggered. The bullet had struck him in the upper arm, shattering it. He cried out as he stumbled forward, but somehow kept his feet and continued to run. The Indians reloaded their muskets, but it was too late for a second chance at the soldier. He was safely back inside the fortification.

The Indians in the cabin screamed their anger at Massy. One of them slammed the front door shut and shoved her back toward the middle of the cabin.

Her warning had saved the soldier's life and the rifle fire alerted the garrison in the fort. But now it appeared that she and her children would pay a terrible price for her actions.

The Miamis' attack strategy was based on a surprise attack that would put the warriors inside the blockhouse before the soldiers could man the barricades. Alishawa had reported to Chief Little Turtle after scouting the location the week before that the terrain surrounding the fortress had been cleared of trees, providing the soldiers an excellent field of fire upon anyone who would dare attack. It was agreed by the Indians planning the strategy that the attack would have to come as a complete surprise.

But now the element of surprise was lost and the raiders knew their mission would fail.

When the Indians realized this, several of them screamed at Massy in a language she did not know, but the message she could understand. A few raised their tomahawks and shook them at her. Massy trembled as she looked at the snarling faces surrounding her. She had acted on impulse and without considering the consequences for her and her children. Now those consequences were all too apparent and she began a silent prayer in anticipation of a quick death for her and the children.

Maumeedoe was on the other side of the cabin, but he suddenly bolted across the cabin floor with his tomahawk raised menacingly above his head. Massy twisted away as he approached and turned her body in an attempt to protect herself and the infant in her arms.

A strong arm gripped her about the shoulders, shoved her away and then a dark hand slipped over her mouth. It was the Indian Alishawa who had stepped in front of Massy to stop Maumeedoe's charge. In perfect English he commanded her, "Be silent."

This stopped Maumeedoe, but only momentarily. Then he resumed the charge, once again aiming his tomahawk for the top of her head. Massy saw the weapon as it came down directly from above her and she tried to pull herself down into her shoulders in a turtle-like defense.

There was a crash above her and then a sudden, piercing pain on the side of her head and cheek. But she wasn't dead.

At the moment that Maumeedoe's tomahawk came crashing down at her head, Alishawa deflected it with his own tomahawk. The blow landed off course, glancing off the left side of Massy's head.

She was stunned and started to lose consciousness. She was not cognizant of Alishawa's strong arm as it encircled her waist and held her upright. Massy looked up at him to see who was holding her, but the room was spinning.

As her consciousness returned, so did the piercing pain in her left cheek and jaw. Her eyes filled with tears and she struggled to maintain her balance and hold on to her son.

Alishawa still had hold of Massy and his strong grip kept her on her feet. Then he shouted to Maumeedoe, "Leave the white woman alone. I will see that she makes no more trouble. I am claiming her as my squaw."

All of this was in the language of the Miamis, and Massy understood none of it. Turning and looking directly at her, Alishawa told her in English that she was now his squaw and that no further harm would come to her.

Massy hardly felt reassured. For the moment, however, she welcomed his warning to the other braves not to harm her. But it did not dull the pain. The side of her head and her cheek throbbed and she had a violent headache. She put her hand to her head and was surprised to find no blood, despite the swelling. She could taste blood inside her mouth, however, as it flowed from her inner cheek where the tomahawk blow had slammed the soft flesh against the teeth.

The full implication of the Indian's statement claiming her as his squaw did not immediately register with Massy. And as her head began to clear she again concentrated on her children's welfare. John was unharmed. Robert was weeping over the punishment that had been inflicted on his mother, as was Samuel who had turned back from the fire in time to see the blow delivered. "But all of us are still alive," Massy thought to herself and she was grateful for that.

Rifle fire could now be heard outside as the garrison mounted the walls of the blockhouse and started to return the Indians' fire. It was too far away for Massy to hear the shouts of the men inside, but she could hear the screams of the Indians as they sought to unnerve the blockhouse defenders.

As she regained her senses Massy again experienced an uneasiness over the plight of Samuel because he was too far from her reach. Once again she motioned for him to come to her side where she was sure the children were safer, particularly since the Indian Alishawa had come to her rescue. She was hoping his defense would include the children.

"Come away from the fire, Samuel, and be with us," she pleaded with him, for now she detected a growing hostility among the Indians to the child's persistence in staying by the fire and his whimpering. The child was testing the patience of all of their captors and she was fearful of what it might lead to if Samuel continued to agitate them.

She turned to Alishawa and pleaded, "Please, let me go to him." The husky, aging warrior would have been willing, but he knew his angry companions would be more inclined to support Maumeedoe's reaction now.

"Stay where you are, squaw," he ordered in a harsh tone.

Massy and her children, however, still were not the center of attention for the Indians. The hostiles concentrated their fire on the blockhouse, even though neither side appeared to be scoring any hits.

Then Massy saw the door to the storehouse near the fort open.

She was shocked. In the middle of this battle a man was standing in the doorway. In the excitement she had forgotten that the blockhouse commissar slept in the storehouse, which was a separate building outside the walls of the blockhouse. And there he was now, a perfect target standing in the storehouse doorway.

He had come out to investigate the rifle fire. As soon as he saw the attacking Indians, however, he broke into a run for the safety of the blockhouse. Several shots were fired at him, but the Indians were as surprised by his appearance as he was with their presence. All of the rifle shots missed him.

Massy was still groggy, but she had enough presence of mind to realize what was happening.

"Run," she murmured, "run hard."

He did. The closest the Indian shots came to hitting him was one bullet that passed through the handkerchief he had wrapped about his head. It tore away some of his hair, but he was otherwise unharmed and managed to reach the blockhouse gate and dart safely inside.

"Oh my God," Massy said, as another figure stepped from inside the storehouse into the doorway. It was the commissar's assistant, who shared the storehouse sleeping quarters. But he certainly didn't share the commissar's good fortune.

His slow reaction to the Indian attack proved to be the last misfortune of his life. As soon as he appeared in the doorway he was a perfect target. The Indians, who were in much closer range now, opened fire. Two of the bullets ripped through the unwary assistant commissar's body and dropped him dead in the storehouse doorway.

Screaming in anticipation, the Indians ran in the dead man's direction with knives and tomahawks at the ready to scalp him.

Angry soldiers at the blockhouse, however, opened fire and their musket fire was sufficient to discourage the attackers. So the Indians retreated out of range.

Massy tried to dismiss her fears and the pain in her head so she could concentrate on the possibility of escape, however remote it seemed. "If the battle continues," she pondered, "perhaps in the confusion their attention will be diverted long enough for me and the children to slip away."

Massy remembered there was a large rock near their cabin, which might provide a place to hide until the Indians departed. But first she had to get out of the cabin and her three children with her.

She tried to create a diversion through conversation with her captors, so she found enough courage to ask several of the Indians who were nearby, "What do you hope to achieve against such a well-armed fortification?"

Everyone seemed to ignore her, except Alishawa.

"How many men are in the blockhouse?" he asked. He wouldn't believe her regardless of what she said, but he wanted to see how crafty a liar Massy could be. It would help to know that before he took her into his lodge as his squaw.

Massy wasn't thinking that far ahead. "There are about forty men inside the walls," she answered. It was a fabrication, for the garrison total was more like twenty. "All of them are excellent marksmen," she added, which was another fabrication. The truth òf the matter was that Massy, who was a gifted marksman, could out-shoot most of the garrison's defenders. She felt some self satisfaction when Alishawa and some of his companions nodded their heads in what Massy believed was an indication that they accepted her statement as fact. As a matter of fact, they didn't believe a word she said.

She didn't see the weak smile on Alishawa's face. He had faced some of these soldiers in battle and knew for a fact that, like his fellow Miamis, very few of the whites could shoot straight. But he wanted to be certain that those who heard Massy's statements were aware that he recognized them as falsehoods. So when Alishawa smiled he turned away from Massy and in the direction of his fellow warriors.

Unfortunately, this created no advantage for Massy and her children. The Indians were aware that without the element of surprise they could not capture the blockhouse. Chief Little Turtle would not be pleased when he learned of this, for the continued presence of the blockhouse would make future raids difficult in this part of the Allegheny River settlements. It would not particularly endear him to Massy Harbison, either, when he learned it was her warning that thwarted the attack.

A messenger was sent to the warriors who had gone forward to fire on the blockhouse to return to the cabin. They were unhappy to do so, but the wisdom of breaking off the engagement was obvious to all of them, even Maumeedoe. So within a few minutes the entire war party was assembled at the Harbison cabin and they made preparations to depart. Massy was consoled that the soldiers in the fort would survive. But there was no consolation in the war party's decision to depart, for it meant there would be no opportunity for her or her children to escape.

At the blockhouse the defenders were relieved that the Indians were breaking off the attack. They shared some guilt, however, that Massy's warning had spared their lives, but may have cost her own life and those of her children.

"Lend me some shells," one defender said to the man beside him. "I'm down to one bullet."

"So am I," came back the reply.

Neither Massy nor the Indians were aware that for some foolish reason ammunition was not stored in the blockhouse, but in the storehouse, and the soldiers had no access to it while under attack. Indeed, most of the defenders were down to a single round in their muskets when the Indians took their leave.

The Miamis were anxious to depart now and ordered Massy with the infant still in her arms and her son Robert to leave the cabin. She had been denied additional clothing earlier, but no attempt was made to discourage her now when she grabbed her cloak near the doorway. Unfortunately for Massy and her children, there were no boots or even sandals near the door as Massy and Robert, clad only in his night shirt, were prodded to walk to the cabin door barefoot.

Standing in the doorway, Massy made one last plea to Samuel to join them. He was still by the fireplace, but now he was tearfully pleading with his mother not to leave him.

The Indians, however, had heard enough.

Several of them started shoving her and Robert to the door. With the wiping sticks used to jam home the powder and shot in their muskets, the Indians flogged Massy every time she stopped to plead for her son.

But it was a useless effort. Finally she wondered if perhaps the Indians would leave Samuel because he had been so much trouble. Certainly no effort was being made to force the child away from the fireplace.

But seeing his mother and brother almost outside of the cabin, Samuel tearfully begged, "Please don't leave."

She called out to him again, pleading with the child to join them. But she was being pulled from the cabin, as was Robert. Then the warrior Maumeedoe suddenly stomped across the floor in the child's direction, shouting his displeasure in words she did not comprehend. She didn't have to. Massy had already learned that Maumeedoe only spoke in anger.

As he neared the child Alishawa stepped in front of him to block his path. He turned to face Samuel and holding out his hand he quietly said, "Come with me, Little Warrior."

He did so because in this bedlam of conflict he wanted to encourage Massy's cooperation by showing the child a kindness. He also hoped to demonstrate to Maumeedoe that there are times when a kindly gesture, especially when dealing with a child, is more effective than anger and harsh words.

Maumeedoe was glaring at Alishawa when he gently took Samuel's hand to lead him away from the fire and to his mother's side. But Samuel, still crying, would have none of it. He twisted away and pulled his hand loose from the Indian's grasp.

Before Alishawa could speak to the child again the irate Maumeedoe stepped forward from behind Alishawa and shoved him aside.

What occurred next was beyond Massy's imagination. The angry warrior reached down and grabbed the boy's ankles. Massy started to plead, "Please don't hurt him, he is just . . ." Before she could say any more, Samuel's little body was jerked off the floor and was swinging through the air in a wide arc. The expression on the child's face was one of total disbelief. Then his head crashed against the threshold. The sound of it startled even the Indians. The skull shattered, spattering brain matter against the door and wall of the cabin.

Massy screamed in disbelief. In her agony her body went reeling, she felt herself falling, and then she lost consciousness.

***

Alishawa was stunned. He had not expected to see a warrior, not even Maumeedoe, brutalize a small child. Had he suspected this would happen he would have stayed between Samuel and Maumeedoe. All he could do now was sympathize with Massy and her pain.

As he glanced about the cabin, however, he saw no evidence that his fellow warriors shared his sentiments. They were surprised, but they were still angry over their failed mission and more interested in leaving in a hurry than in chastising their ill-tempered companion.

***

How long she remained unconscious, Massy did not know. But she came out of that state when a hard blow was delivered by one of the Indians across her head and face. This restored her to her senses and the unbelievable reality of the butchery she had just witnessed on her beloved son.

In falling, she also had lost her grip on John. She realized he was on the floor beside her and once again was crying. Also in shock over what he had just seen, Robert began to mumble his murdered brother's name amidst tears and moans. But the butchery wasn't over. Incredibly, Maumeedoe then knelt down by Samuel's lifeless form and swiftly cut away the child's battered scalp.

Massy felt nauseous and turned her head away. She held her wailing infant tightly in her arms for fear that he soon would suffer the same fate. She also wanted to put a protective arm around Robert. But he was out of reach and the Indians were in no mood to accommodate tenderness. So Massy, carrying her infant son and followed by Robert, was forced out of the cabin. While still dazed over the horrifying events of this morning, they were led away from the Harbison homestead.

The cabin disappeared too soon from their vision as the Indians led them into the nearby woods and eventually down to the Allegheny River. There they walked single file along the top of the river bank.

Alishawa plodded along in silence. Maumeedoe's butchery would make it that much more difficult for him to convert his new squaw to the ways of the Miami women. That task would be difficult, for this obviously was a woman of spirit, but she would have to leave her white ways and become a Miami squaw. He needed her, not only for the beauty and warmth she would bring to his cold lodge, but for the sons he was now certain he would sire with her.

Massy was in total misery as she followed the Indians. Her head and face hurt. She was frightened for herself and her two sons. Her heart ached for her third little boy who was so viciously murdered before her eyes.

Alishawa obviously was not the defender she thought he might be, for he seemed helpless during the massacre of her son.

"And what would become of the infant within me?" she wondered. "If I live and he is born in an Indian camp will he also be subjected to the inhumane abuse I witnessed this morning?" Massy's thoughts bounced from one ugly scene to another. Her head ached and her bare feet were a new source of pain as she walked over rough terrain and felt the pricks and jabs of the thorns and briars in her path.

Any hopes for rescue were quickly fading as the distance grew between her and the home she was sure she never would see again. Massy was desperate and her thoughts now turned to God as she silently pleaded for divine intervention. She could find no peace or reassurance in her prayers, however, because the image of Samuel's bloody murder kept crowding out all other thoughts. When a second thought did come to mind, it was in the form of a question.

"How soon will it be before we all suffer a similar fate?"

Massy was unaware of the passing of time, so she wasn't sure how long it was before the Indians stopped and began to divide the plunder from the Harbison cabin. Most of the household items that had been taken had been personally brought into the home by her, and in her mind she could place each item's setting back in the cabin as it was pulled from the sack and brandished about. But for Massy these material things had lost all value.

This pause in their march gave Massy the opportunity to make a quick count of the number in the raiding party. She counted thirty-two. Their heads had been plucked free of hair, except for the strands that were tied into a scalp lock in the back. They wore the buckskin breechcloth, but were bare chested with a powder horn hanging from a shoulder strap. Either moccasins or deerskin leggings covered their lower extremities.

Massy was certain that two in the raiding party were white men who were dressed and painted as Indians. She couldn't help but wonder why and then concluded they must be renegades, men with a price on their heads, who fled civilization and joined the natives.

Several of the Indians spoke English when they conversed with the two white men, but none as clearly as Alishawa. She also recognized some of them from their canoe trips up and down the Allegheny River.

Two in the group appeared to be Seneca Indians and she was certain that another pair were from the Munsees tribe. Massy knew this because she had seen them come to the shop near the blockhouse to have their guns repaired. The rest of the party, she presumed, were Miamis.

***

Both Maumeedoe and Alishawa ignored the loot. Maumeedoe was still filled with anger over the failed attack on the blockhouse, and he knew who was responsible for that. Alishawa regretted that they would have to report failure to Little Turtle and he knew the chief would resent the presence in his village of the white woman who caused it. He also knew Maumeedoe would probably want to make a case for torturing the woman as punishment for her indiscretion.

Chief Little Turtle, however, liked Alishawa, even though he was not a fearsome warrior. He had served the chief well in his earlier years when his talent for mastering languages enabled Little Turtle to communicate with other Indian tribes. In fact, it was Alishawa's gift as an interpreter that prompted Little Turtle to appoint him as liaison with their allies, the troops from Great Britain, during the Revolutionary War.

He had learned to speak the Englishmen's tongue quite fluently and had enjoyed long periods of privileged existence at the English Army quarters in Detroit while he mastered the language. He also had developed a taste for English women while in Detroit, although it was beauty he was compelled to enjoy from afar. He knew that if he attempted to make friends with one of these British ladies it would be resented and he could have been sent packing back to Little Turtle. So he kept his distance, learned the language and occasionally daydreamed about someday having a better opportunity to befriend a white woman.

His discretion paid off handsomely. When he returned to Little Turtle as an accomplished interpreter of the English language he was welcomed into the councils of war and required to sit at Little Turtle's side during all such meetings. The chief was particularly appreciative of Alishawa's talents when there was an occasion to meet with a British officer who was unaware of Alishawa's interpretive skills and made uncomplimentary comments about the Miamis to his assistants in the belief that these Indians were unaware.

Alishawa would rely on that relationship with Little Turtle to overcome the rantings and ravings of this warrior, Maumeedoe, whom most Indians considered too reckless to rely on in a fight.

***

They had hardly resumed their journey when they came upon several horses in a makeshift corral. Massy recognized them as belonging to her uncle, John Currie. The Indians took immediate possession of them.

Now that they had mounts they thought there might still be an opportunity for the war party to attack some of the other Allegheny River settlements before the settlers learned about this day's raid. It was decided, therefore, that the prisoners would only slow them down, so Alishawa was told to take charge of Massy and her sons and lead them back to the camp northwest of Fort Pitt where they had agreed to rendezvous before heading back to their village on the west Ohio river that the whites called St. Mary. One other warrior was assigned to accompany Alishawa on this journey to provide assistance. It was Maumeedoe.

Being made to work together was an assignment neither Indian preferred. But the assignments made sense to the others. Alishawa was not a great asset in a fight because of his minimal fighting skills and the limitations his thirty-eight years imposed on his less-than-perfect body. Courageous and fierce though he was as a fighter, Maumeedoe was too prone to mistakes that jeopardized everyone because of his unquenchable thirst for white men's scalps.

As the rest of the war party started off in another direction, Alishawa directed Massy to mount one of the animals. He offered his assistance because she was holding an infant in her arms, took the child from her while she climbed astride the horse and then returned him.

As Alishawa returned the infant to her, Massy nodded to indicate her appreciation. She was not in a gracious mood, but any kindness under these circumstances was welcome. It also was a relief to get off her battered feet. The Indian turned and tethered the horse to his mount. Before leaving Massy's side, however, he turned back and spoke to her in a subdued voice.

"My name is Alishawa," he said. "He is Maumeedoe. As you saw, he is crazy. I regret what he did to your boy, but be careful not to anger him. He is irresponsible."

Massy was impressed with the Indian's excellent English. She never expected to hear one converse so well in her own language. "Where did he learn to speak English so well?" she wondered.

Meanwhile Maumeedoe had climbed up on the third horse, then pulled Robert up with him.

With everyone mounted, Alishawa led the captives further up the river in the direction of the Kiskiminetas River. Maumeedoe had a bag full of plunder in one hand and over one shoulder he carried a large powder horn. It had become awkward to handle since the war party had departed the Harbison cabin, but the burden was more manageable now that he could ride.

Escape, while becoming less likely, was still in Massy's thoughts and she was certain that Robert was thinking the same in spite of his age. But she had seen the viciousness of the Indians' wrath in the murder of Samuel and knew she could not afford to be reckless. As her horse plodded on behind Alishawa's mount she wondered if somewhere along the path they might come across armed settlers who would fire on the Indians and rescue them. That likelihood was slim, she knew, and growing slimmer the more distance they traveled. But it gave Massy something to cling to as she struggled to cope with the unbelievable events of this day.

3
More Barbarism

The riders rode in silence as they headed east and followed the path of the Allegheny River. With the increasing unfamiliarity of the terrain, Massy was losing her sense of where they were, and that was disconcerting to her should she somehow manage to get free. She expected at some point they would cross the river to its north shore because the residents of the frontier communities along the Allegheny River considered the north side of the river Indian country.

What she was not aware of was that Alishawa and Maumeedoe were trying to retrace the steps the war party had taken when it crossed the river under cover of darkness that previous night. The Miami tribesmen were familiar with the Ohio River settlements on the western side of Pittsburgh. But the land east of Pittsburgh on the Allegheny River was relatively new to them. Having made the crossing at night didn't make it any easier to find their way back. It occurred to her that perhaps their unfamiliarity with the terrain explained the presence of the Seneca and Munsee Indians in the raiding party.

A small island in the middle of the river was the landmark they were looking for because it was the easiest crossing point. There was only a narrow channel between the north shore and the island when the river was low and Alishawa and Maumeedoe knew the water was shallow enough at one location to allow them to wade ashore from the island. The distance between the island and the south shore where they were traveling was much greater and the channel was too deep to traverse without a canoe.

The Indians had concealed their canoes in the underbrush along the shore when they disembarked the previous night, so Alishawa and Maumeedoe knew the canoes would be there for them if they located the correct crossing point.

Massy's concern was less about where they were going, and more about what would happen once they got there . . . if they got there. And the more distance they put between them and her home the more frightened and discouraged she became. Prayer had been a consistent part of her days as a child in New Jersey and into her adult life. When she prayed in the past, however, it frequently was just monotonous repetition of formal prayer. But not now. Now she was making a silent, personal plea to the Almighty to lead her and her sons out of this hell in which they were trapped before it was too late.

The ugly images of the day's events kept recurring in her thoughts, making it difficult for Massy to concentrate on her prayer in spite of her fervor. It was her only thread of hope, however thin a thread it was, but it was all she had now.

It also was of no small concern to Massy that Robert was riding on the same horse with Maumeedoe, the savage who so ruthlessly killed Samuel. It became even more disconcerting when his mount periodically dropped back almost out of sight. He did so to determine if they were being followed. But it also meant that Robert could be in greater peril. "They must have believed me when I told them there were so many soldiers at the blockhouse," she told herself, "and now they are scouting the back trail for a possible rescue party."

But Massy knew it would be difficult for rescuers to be sent after her and her sons. If anything, the garrison was undermanned. And even if the soldiers could manage to undertake such a search, she knew in all probability they would ultimately follow the footprints left by the larger raiding party rather than pursue the smaller tracks left by three horses.

Relying on rescue under these circumstances, Massy knew, was hoping for a miracle. She knew that she and her sons were very much alone with these two hostiles.

Discouraged and frightened as she was, she kept reminding herself to remain alert should there suddenly be an opportunity to escape. "Fantasizing won't help, " she told herself, "but stay alert."

When her thoughts drifted to Samuel now she knew she had to set them aside and concentrate on survival. This was not the proper time to mourn her murdered son. Instead she devised her own prayerful plea .

"Please, God, tenderly enfold Samuel in your loving arms and welcome him into eternity."

"No, no, no," Massy told herself each time tears threatened to stain her cheeks. She was determined not to show any weakness to her captors.

But this did not dull her sorrow that never again would she hear Samuel's childish laugh, his tearful cries, or the child's pleas for his mother's caring assistance. For now she knew she must store these memories and the tears until she could mourn her son at a more fitting time and place.

***

From the moment Maumeedoe and Alishawa separated from the main party Massy tried to concentrate on her captors to see if they had any apparent weaknesses. Alishawa obviously was not a vicious savage. She remembered that he did try to rescue Samuel in the cabin, but he seemed helpless to follow through when Maumeedoe shoved him aside and killed her son.

The older Indian appeared to be in charge. But Massy was aware that the younger Maumeedoe was a sturdier, younger figure as well as a vicious killer. She also remembered that Alishawa called him "crazy" and warned her not to rile him. "I won't," she told herself, "if I can possibly avoid it."

As for Alishawa, he had taken her from the cabin because he wanted her to be his squaw. This thought was troubling enough. But what would become of her sons? Did he have plans for them as well, or even more frightening to contemplate, did he have no plans for them?

She guessed that Alishawa was in his late thirties. He was broad-shouldered, but he was equally thick at the hips and his stomach was beginning to slide over the belt he wore. He was several inches under six feet, his face was lined and his black hair was showing streaks of gray. In his best younger days he would not have been handsome because his nose was too large.

Massy had to be impressed, however, with his command of the English language. Obviously he knew more than just a few phrases. Indeed, Massy wouldn't be surprised if he could read and write.

Maumeedoe was a study in opposites. Each time she observed him he was scowling.

"What would be our fate," she wondered, "if something happened to the older Indian and our lives were suddenly in his murdering hands?" The answer was obvious. Death would be imminent.

"But would it be swift or slow and painful?" She suspected the latter, for Massy had heard that Indians delighted in measuring out the pain they inflicted in small, excruciating doses. She knew this from the comments of her husband and other frontiersmen when discussing how Indians tortured their captives, and Massy had no reason to disbelieve them. She frequently overheard John Harbison and the lodgers in their cabin late at night discussing the evidence of torture they had come upon in abandoned Indian camps.

It also was known on the frontier that some Indians frequently mutilated captives in an effort to inflict maximum pain. They would chop off fingers and toes. Ultimately they might cut away the other body extremities or put the captives to the torch.

"Could I endure such agony?" she wondered. Obviously not, for even the thought of it was difficult to endure. And what of her children? Would they also be tortured and would she be compelled to watch it?

Massy tried to dismiss these ugly thoughts. They only served to unnerve her and make her otherwise unfit to meet whatever crisis might await them. But the constant presence of Maumeedoe made them hard to dismiss.

His size and his physique made him an imposing figure. He was well over six feet, lean with an abundance of young man's muscle in his biceps, chest and back. Unlike Alishawa, his stomach was flat.

There was nothing special about his facial features, except that his scowl seemed permanent and made his appearance constantly fearsome. This warrior obviously found satisfaction in his vicious behavior.

***

Although she had lost track of the passing of time, Massy was certain several hours had passed because the sun was now sliding into the west. More troubling to her was the total unfamiliarity of the country they were now passing through. Massy thought she knew the Allegheny River well because she had lived near it for the past few years. But this was a part of the river she never had seen before and the river itself had never before appeared so cold and unfriendly.

The river bank they had been following now sloped in a steep incline toward the river's edge. Alishawa stopped his horse and held up his hand for the others to do likewise, then motioned for Maumeedoe to join him.

He was staring out into the river where there was a small island when Maumeedoe guided his horse past Massy's mount and rode up to Alishawa.

"I think this is where we crossed the river last night," Alishawa said to Maumeedoe. "I would like to take the horses with us. They can help us travel faster once we cross the river. Besides, they may be needed to help the others carry whatever they bring from raiding the other white settlements."

Maumeedoe was silent, but nodded his head in agreement.

Massy made no effort to hear what her captors were discussing. Even if she could it would not have helped because she didn't understand the Miami language. Sitting silently behind Maumeedoe, Robert also showed no interest in the conversation.

"How lonely and frightened he looks," Massy thought to herself. Under other circumstances he would have been thrilled to be riding on a horse. All frontier boys longed to learn to ride. But not under these conditions.

"I'll ride down the slope first with the boy," Maumeedoe told Alishawa. "Send the woman and child down at the same time."

Alishawa resented Maumeedoe's assumption of authority, but he was more surprised at his companion's recklessness. "It is too steep to ride down," he cautioned. "Dismount and lead the horse down with the boy on it."

Maumeedoe stared at Alishawa, but said nothing. Massy, however, detected that the two of them were having a disagreement from the expressions on their faces and the tone of voice. She only wished there was something she could do or say that would further aggravate their dispute.

Alishawa looked upon Maumeedoe's intention to ride the horse down the slope as another example of his careless bravado. His disgust turned to anger a moment later when Maumeedoe, after pointing his mount down the slope, turned to Massy and indicated with his hand that she should follow.

Alishawa specifically did not want Massy to follow Maumeedoe, for he was afraid she would be injured in a fall. He didn't know it, but that wasn't likely. Massy had sufficient knowledge of horses to realize this was folly. She glared after Maumeedoe and then emphatically told him "NO." Massy knew a safe descent would be nearly impossible while the rider remained astride the horse because the slope was too steep for the horse to maintain its balance. But she was more concerned about the danger to her son from Maumeedoe's foolish decision.

Something else occurred to her. Perhaps Indians were not as wilderness-wise as she had been led to believe, at least not these two. "Certainly this younger Indian is not," she told herself.

Maumeedoe grunted and again pointed the way for Massy to follow as his mount started down to the river's edge. Alishawa just stared at the two of them, but said nothing. Defiance now rising within her, Massy called out, "That is stupid." And with that she dismounted, took her infant son John firmly in the grasp of her right arm, and with her free hand started walking the horse down the slope.

Alishawa was silent, but he couldn't mask his enjoyment over Maumeedoe's anger and Massy's demonstration of defiance. In fact, he was hoping she would reach the river bank before Maumeedoe. He knew that would make his fellow tribesman look even more foolish.

But now he was watching Massy lead her mount and found himself admiring her skill, particularly while holding a baby in the other arm. "This is a woman of great spirit," he concluded, and congratulated himself on choosing her to be his squaw.

Maumeedoe was not amused, either by Massy's defiance or her unexpected skill with a horse. His mutterings were in his native tongue, but Massy was aware of his irritation by the angry sound of his voice. She pretended to ignore him, but inwardly it gave her some satisfaction that she was able to rile this enemy.

Paying too much attention to Massy and not enough to the maneuverings of the horse he was astride, Maumeedoe suddenly felt the horse starting to slide out beneath him. He pulled back on the rein, but this didn't help and the horse lost its footing.

"You're losing the horse!" Alishawa shouted. "Jump free of it with the boy." But the warning came too late. The horse begin to fall.

"Noooo!" Massy screamed as the horse's legs started to slide out from beneath it and the riders were in danger of falling under the animal. She released her mount and tried to reach Robert. But the slope was too slippery and Maumeedoe's mount was sliding away from her.

Maumeedoe and Robert had been slow to react, but now the boy recognized the danger. "Help me, Mother," she heard him cry out, and then the horse slid out from under Maumeedoe and Robert and went tumbling down to the river's edge. The riders had fallen free of the mount, but they also slid down the bank right after the horse until they reached the river's edge. Massy watched all this helplessly, hoping that her Robert would escape unharmed and that the Indian would break something, preferably his neck.

Their bodies were now partly submerged in the water with the horse, but it was obvious that no serious injury had resulted. Massy was relieved when Robert scrambled to his feet. He was trembling and crying over the bruises suffered in the fall, but that was the extent of the damage.

His captor also was unhurt, but he could not hide his embarrassment. Atop the bank, once he saw that no one was injured, Alishawa could not contain himself. He was laughing, loudly, as he dismounted and started to descend the slope and lead his mount behind him. Maumeedoe failed to see the humor as he rose to his feet and began brushing himself off. Robert's tears didn't help his disposition, so he snatched the boy's arm with force. Robert winced and fell to his knees, while the pain from Maumeedoe's stern grip made him cry all the more.

Angry over his gruff manner in handling the boy, Massy screamed at Maumeedoe when she saw Robert crying. "You have no cause to hurt the child," she shouted. "It was your foolishness that caused the horse to fall."

Maumeedoe didn't understand a word Massy said, but he got the message and he didn't like it.

Alishawa was still leading his horse down the slope with no apparent difficulty when Massy started toward her son to comfort him. But Maumeedoe was in no mood for tender loving care at this moment. He stepped between Massy and Robert with a menacing glare and ordered her back.

Now Massy wondered what was their purpose in climbing down the bank with the horses.

"Surely they are not going to attempt to forge the river against the current on horseback," she said to herself. Massy knew she could not handle a horse in water that deep and a one-year-old infant in her arms.

The Indians had another option. They intended to steer the horses into the river and have them swim across to the island.

Maumeedoe forced Robert to walk toward Alishawa. "You hold him," he said, "and I will get a canoe." Then he turned, walked into the shallows of the river and waded knee-deep to a collection of loose rocks jutting out from the bank. Climbing over the rocks, he disappeared for a few moments. When he reappeared he was pushing one of the bark canoes the war party had hidden there.

Massy could see now there were other canoes hidden behind the rocks and correctly assumed this was how the Indians came to attack their settlement after hiding the canoes when they landed at this location. She made a mental note so she could relay this information to her husband or other settlers. Then she remembered that in all probability she never would have the opportunity to share this with them.

Buffalo Creek joined the Allegheny River on the opposite shore and Massy could see it from where she stood. While she had never before seen this section of the river, she recognized the creek from earlier descriptions given by her husband.

Alishawa and Maumeedoe were anxious to get across the river. "In," Alishawa ordered Massy as he pointed to the canoe. Maumeedoe was less formal with Robert. He picked the boy up and deposited him in the vessel none too gently.

Now Alishawa was trying to force the horses to enter the river and swim, which Massy knew the horses would not do. So the three mounts stood motionless on the shore and refused to venture into the water.

Alishawa and Maumeedoe quickly grew impatient. They would wait no longer. "Let us just leave them here," Alishawa told Maumeedoe, and he agreed.

Three horses were left stranded at the river's edge. This lack of foresight, however, was not lost on Massy. "Don't they know riderless horses are most unlikely to enter a river where the water is over their heads?" she wondered. "Why did they go to such trouble to lead the horses down the river bank, only to abandon them at the water's edge?" she asked herself. Surely it made no sense.

This revelation, plus the war party's decision to send these two Indians off with a woman prisoner and two children while the rest went off to conduct more raids, was puzzling to Massy. "Is there a message in this?" she pondered. Was it a reflection of the other Indians' lack of respect for what Alishawa and Maumeedoe could contribute in their raids on other settlements?

All five passengers were seated in the canoe now and they shoved off for the island. Massy forgot about the ineptitude of her captors as they made their way across the river. Her principal concern now was that any hope of rescue would be left behind on the southern shore of the Allegheny River and that with every stroke of the paddles the canoe was delivering her and her children deeper and deeper into captivity.

Should they survive the journey, she surmised, the life facing them in an Indian village would likely be extremely harsh. Until now Massy had refused to consider this possibility. "But now it appears to be the most likely," she told herself.

Massy had been dismissing the image in her mind of surrendering herself as a squaw to a savage. It was unbearably repulsive. But it now seemed most likely. The thought became uglier when she realized she never would be able to disassociate Alishawa from the brutal murder of her helpless son. Even though he had tried to intervene on the child's behalf, she knew none of this would have happened if Alishawa and the other Miamis had not entered the Harbison cabin.

"By his very presence," she reminded herself, "he was a part of that bloodthirsty raiding party."

"But what choice will I really have if I am in captivity?" Massy asked herself. "I won't be able to fight it and what will be my fate if I refuse? Rape? Torture? And in the end, a brutal death?"

The alternative was submission, and Massy could not imagine herself surrendering to this under any circumstance.

"I will have to choose death. Should that day come I will summon the courage to refuse and accept the consequences."

But would she have the courage when the time came? Massy wasn't certain.

These gruesome thoughts of death were new for this frontier woman, particularly one so young. But so much had changed in her life in just a few hours, none of it wholesome, so somehow thoughts of her death belonged.

"If I die, what will be the fate of my sons and what of the child still within me?" she was compelled to ponder. "Will they in time become savages like their captors or will they also die at the hands of the Indians as punishment for their white skin?"

The nose of the canoe ground into the soft turf of the island. The sudden stop jolted Massy back into the present. The two Indians wasted no time, leaping from the canoe and guiding it onto land. Massy, with the infant in her arms, and Robert were ordered out. Robert got out first and came to his mother's side to hold John while she stepped onto the turf.

While Alishawa and Maumeedoe dragged the canoe away from the shore and busied themselves with hiding it beneath some underbrush, Massy and Robert seized this first moment they had to be alone since their capture and they embraced. She quickly examined his bruises from the fall down the river bank and was grateful they were only brush burns. But being held tenderly in his mother's arms after what he had been through this day was too comforting for Robert and he started to cry.

Massy knew she only had a brief moment to be alone with him. "I know it hurts, but you must stop crying," she cautioned Robert. She didn't want his tears to irritate their captors as Samuel's crying had done. "Remember what they did to Samuel when he cried," she warned him. But that was a mistake. Bringing up Samuel's name made Robert sob all the more.

Maumeedoe looked up from the canoe-hiding chore and discovered the mother and son reunion. He screamed as he rushed up to them and shoved them apart.

"I only want to see if he is all right," Massy protested. But Maumeedoe's anger would not be so easily dismissed. In an effort to avoid any unpleasantness, Alishawa walked up to Massy and told her, "Bring the infant and follow me to the other side of the island."

She was relieved to look back and see Robert and Maumeedoe following them, but the thought of Robert walking behind her in the company of Maumeedoe and out of her sight still was a cause for concern. Robert continued to sob, so after they had gone a short distance Massy glanced over her shoulder again and immediately regretted it.

Maumeedoe's tomahawk was coming down on Robert's head behind the full force of the Indian's powerful arm. Before the stunned Massy could speak there was an ugly cracking sound as the tomahawk crushed the top of the unsuspecting child's head.

Massy screamed as she reached for Robert, but she was too late. The crown of his head took the full force of the tomahawk blow, his body went limp as he pitched forward, arms flailing out at his sides, and from his head came a crimson flow.

The crumpled form was face down on the ground when Massy reached him. But before she could wrap him in her arms, she felt her body in the tight grip of Alishawa. He pulled her and John back and put his hand over her mouth to keep her silent. He was fearful that Massy's head would be Maumeedoe's next target and this was an effort to get her out of harm's way.

He was not, however, expecting Maumeedoe's next move when he quickly discarded the tomahawk and pulled out his scalping knife.

Alishawa raised his hand in an effort to stop him, but it was too late. Maumeedoe was quite gifted at quickly salvaging scalps, which he was about to do. Massy realized what he was going to do and lunged at Maumeedoe to protect her son's seemingly lifeless form. But Maumeedoe's weapon already was flashing in the sun as he pulled the child's head back with one hand, sliced quickly around the bloody scalp and then yanked the scalp free of the crown.

"You butcher!" she screamed as she tried to break free of Alishawa's hold. But he would not let her go, certainly not while Maumeedoe still had a sharp knife in his hand. Massy fell forward from her kneeling position in shock and disbelief and then she lost consciousness.

***

When Massy's body went limp, Alishawa let her down to the ground and then came up to Maumeedoe. His anger was quite apparent. "Why did you kill the boy?" he shouted. "He was no trouble. Now because of this we will be delayed in reaching the other shore."

"I should kill all of them," the angry Maumeedoe answered him as he turned loose Robert's bloody head and wiped the knife clean against Robert's body.

"You are crazy," Alishawa replied. "If we wanted them killed we would have done it in the cabin. These are not warriors. They are our captives, a helpless woman and her children. What harm could they bring you?"

"These helpless children grow up to be soldiers who kill our women and children or settlers who steal our land. Their women breed them." He had dropped his musket to the ground in order to wield the tomahawk and knife, so the musket was out of his reach. Alishawa's musket was in his hand and ready to fire and for a brief moment he wanted to use it on this bloodthirsty warrior. "But what good would it do now?" he asked himself. "The child is already dead."

***

Alishawa and all of the Miamis knew the reason for Maumeedoe's bloodthirsty acts. At the age of twelve he was out with a hunting party when the American soldiers suddenly rode into their village setting lodges ablaze and indiscriminately shooting or bayoneting the occupants. There were only a few warriors in the village at the time. The rest were off fighting with their British allies. What the soldiers found in the lodges were old men, women and children. And they slaughtered them.

Maumeedoe arrived back with the hunting party not long after the soldiers departed. The carnage that greeted him was a scene he never would forget. Indians of all ages and both sexes were strewn about the village, most of them already dead. A few unfortunate ones were still breathing. Blood was everywhere.

A year later his own father was taken prisoner near Fort Washington. At first it was thought he was being held prisoner for the purpose of exchange for white prisoners. But when the war ended he didn't come back in a prisoner exchange. He had died or was killed in a white prison camp and was buried there.

Motivation for Maumeedoe's hatred of the white enemy was understood by all of the Miamis. Nevertheless, his recklessness in battle was a concern to all.

***

When Massy collapsed, John had fallen from her grasp. He was left there protesting the sudden loss of his mother's protective arms while Alishawa and Maumeedoe argued about the killing of Robert.

Alishawa picked John up as Massy was regaining consciousness and told Maumeedoe, "Get the body out of sight before she awakes. The longer we stay on this island the likelier it is we will be discovered." Maumeedoe complied, for he also wanted to get to the north shore of the river. But he forgot to remove the scalp.

When Massy regained her senses and started looking about for her infant child, the first sight to register with her was the savage Maumeedoe standing near her and still clutching Robert's bloody scalp.

She had risen to her knees, but at this sight she fell forward once more. Maumeedoe had enough of her grieving, so he grabbed Massy by the hair and started beating her about her body with his fists and demanding that she rise to her feet.

Alishawa shoved Maumeedoe away from Massy. She was in such a state of shock, however, the blows had not registered with her. Nor was she aware of Alishawa coming to her rescue.

"Dear Jesus," she prayed aloud, "please take me, too. This sorrow is beyond bearing." The Indians' patience was at an end, however, and both of them shouted warnings. Maumeedoe kicked her leg and threatened more severe treatment if she didn't rise to her feet immediately. Alishawa's warning was more out of fear over what else Maumeedoe might do in his rage. The Indians were shouting in their native tongue. What Massy didn't know was that while Maumeedoe was aiming his threats at her, Alishawa was warning him.

Now Massy heard John's whimpering cries. Alishawa had him in his hands and handed him to her. She took the baby in her arms and gently hugged him to her bosom. This morning she was the mother of three boys. Now all she had was a one-year-old and memories.

The Indians realized that Massy was still in shock even though she managed to get to her feet. So they walked her to the water's edge and then out into the river until it was knee deep. While Alishawa held young John, he and Maumeedoe took turns pouring water from cupped hands over her head. The treatment worked. When she was restored to her senses Massy looked about for John and took him back in her arms. Then she glanced at Maumeedoe. Her murdered son's scalp was nowhere in sight, nor was Robert's body.

The Indians prodded Massy to move on and they walked to the other side of the island. They were looking for a shallow channel that they knew was there, which would permit them to wade across to the north shore of the river. After a period of searching Alishawa located the channel and signaled to Maumeedoe to come with Massy and her child. This decision to abandon the canoe and proceed on foot momentarily distracted Massy from her grief. The raiding party obviously had come down the Allegheny by canoe. So it puzzled her that her captors would now chose to return on foot. Perhaps the current was too strong, she surmised, for two men to paddle upstream with a woman and a baby as passengers. But now it worried Massy that perhaps their reasons for crossing to the opposite shore were more devious.

As they stepped to the water's edge, she suddenly felt the sturdy but unfriendly grip of Maumeedoe's hand on her shoulder. He thrust her forward into the cold waters of the Allegheny River. She wanted to keep her cloak dry, but this was impossible with John in her arms. So she endured the cold and proceeded to step further out into the chilly waters. Massy couldn't help but wonder if her captors intended to drown her, for she felt their presence on each side of her. But they had no such intentions. Because of the depth there, Massy was compelled to hold John above her head in order to keep him dry. Somewhat surprisingly, the Indians assisted her by lifting her up under the armpits as they crossed the shallows to the opposite bank.

When she was on land again Massy glanced back at the now faraway southern shore of the Allegheny River. This was the last boundary between her civilization and the savage world she was now entering. Was she seeing it for the last time? Most likely. Would she ever see her husband and friends again? Hardly.

Massy began to surrender to despair. She was filled with foreboding for herself, her one-year-old surviving son and the unborn child within her. She had no option but to quietly and obediently plod along the path between Alishawa and Maumeedoe, and despair was unavoidable. But that emotion was accompanied by a strong hate growing within her for the savage who had murdered Samuel and Robert. Massy's Christianity demanded forgiveness. She had not forgotten that. But at this moment she could not honestly embrace it. Unashamedly she also found herself hoping that Maumeedoe would someday be subjected to the same vicious death as he had brought down on her sons.

The trip through the waters of the Allegheny had added a new misery to Massy's aches and pains. The cloak she wore and the flimsy nightgown beneath it were soaked. With the sun fading, the absence of its warm rays only magnified the chill she felt from the wet clothes.

She started to remove the cloak, for it was soaking wet and only added to her discomfort. As she did, however, she discovered that the bottom of her petticoat was in rags and that her bare legs were exposed almost to the hip. She put the cloak around her shoulders again and covered herself as best she could.

Young John had survived the crossing in good health. Still dry and safely settled in his mothers arms, he slipped into a quiet slumber as they set out again. Massy wondered what would happen to John if the Indians decided to murder her on the trail. Most likely it would be the end for her infant as well.

The woods grew darker as daylight took its leave. They had traveled only a short distance when they arrived at Big Buffalo Creek. Alishawa and Maumeedoe intended to ford this stream, but it was flowing too rapidly to permit crossing where they stood. So once more they began to search along the creek bank for a shallow section. Since this was only a creek, however, finding a shallow passageway was not difficult. After walking upstream a short distance Maumeedoe pointed into the creek and across to the other side.

"Come now," Alishawa told her, "we will help you across." He had meant it to be reassuring. But it wasn't. With that the two warriors again lifted her up by the armpits and led her across the stream to the other side.

With her body once again submerged in cold water Massy experienced more chills, so by the time they reached the other side of the creek and climbed its bank she was cold and weary and desperately in need of rest. It also occurred to her that she had not eaten this day, although at this point food had no appeal to her.

But rest was not on the Indians' agenda, at least not now. When Massy tried to sit down Maumeedoe put both hands under her shoulder and yanked her upwards. He said nothing, but Alishawa cautioned her, "This is not the time to rest." So they led Massy further into the wilderness while she clutched John a little closer to her bosom.

Massy pondered the possibility that she wouldn't last the night. Impatient with the disruptions and slowed by a child-carrying mother, perhaps her captors in their haste to distance themselves from any possible pursuers would kill them both and end their troubles. Because of her despondency, the thought no longer frightened her.

***

Arriving safely on the north shore of the Allegheny River was a joyous occasion for Alishawa. He felt safe in this part of the wilderness and now was certain he would bring Massy back to his lodge in the Miami village where he would be the envy of his comrades.

Alishawa was anticipating more than just the jealous glances of his fellow tribesmen. It had been his desire since he was a young man to father sons. That goal had eluded him so far. He had no children by his first squaw and two daughters from the second.

He had taken the first squaw while in his late teens. But she was not fertile. For four years they tried unsuccessfully to have children, but it was all to no avail. Then a smallpox plague swept through the village while he was accompanying Little Turtle to a conference of several tribes and his woman died without ever going through childbirth.

He now had another squaw, but all she bore him were two daughters. He still wanted sons, but at his age he was running out of time.

This comely white woman would solve his problems, he was certain. She had nothing but boys. Perhaps, he thought, once she learns the ways of the Miamis she would understand and willingly help him achieve that goal.

Alishawa, wise in many ways, had clearly misread the temperament of the woman he now held hostage.

***

In growing darkness Massy was having a difficult time walking. Then her foot struck a jagged rock and the piercing pain made her stop and reach down to rub away the pain in her toe. When she glanced down she was surprised to see blood smears around her toes and pieces of thorns sticking out from the sides of her feet. They had been so cold from being in the water that she had not felt the brambles and thorns puncturing her flesh. She felt them now, however, and each new step was another experience in pain.

"Dear God," she silently asked, "how much more can I take?"

4
Death Wish

Massy's head still ached from the tomahawk blow in the cabin that morning and her jaw, swollen from the same blow, was sore and immovable. Having just walked through the cold waters of the Allegheny River and Big Buffalo Creek, her clothes were soaked and she was shivering in the cold. The numbness in her bare feet after walking through the water was wearing off and making her aware once more of the battering they had endured. She also was weak from no nourishment that day, which combined with the weariness from the long march, also made her nauseous. The greatest pain, however, was in her heart as images of her slain children kept coming into focus.

"If I should survive all of this," she asked herself, "what do I have to look forward to?" She knew all too well that the answer was a life of abuse and degradation in an Indian village as the property of an Indian.

Massy did not like the conclusion where this train of thought led....that the only way out was to die. But there it was and it seemed undeniably true.

She was sinking into a sea of depression with her every thought, whether they were about her captors, herself, the infant son in her arms, or the unborn within her. There was no cause for hope. Massy just could not accept an existence she would be compelled to endure as a captive. Such a life would be beyond bearing.

"Please," she implored God, "free me from this nightmare."

The slayings of Samuel and Robert, Massy decided, were the spontaneous reactions of one savage. In his frustration over the failure to capture the blockhouse, Maumeedoe struck down one frightened child who irritated him. He killed the second after he and Robert had an embarrassing fall from a horse down the river bank and the child's tearful response to that incident. "So when events don't go as Maumeedoe expects he is provoked," Massy told herself, "and acts extremely irrational."

Because of Maumeedoe's demonstrated ill temperament, Massy concluded that he would be the most likely to bring a swift death down upon her if he were provoked. And she would soon have the opportunity to test that conclusion. Since their arrival at the river's north shore the Indians, without the horses, were by necessity carrying the loot they had taken from the Harbison cabin. They had not walked far from Big Buffalo Creek, therefore, when Maumeedoe lightened his burden by forcing Massy to carry the large powder horn he had slung over his shoulder.

He did this without any explanation, just by suddenly removing the horn from his shoulder and sliding it over her shoulder. But while he did this in silence, the grim expression on his face made it clear to Massy he would tolerate no objections.

With a one-year-old son in one arm, however, it was not an easy burden for Massy to shoulder. She reacted in anger, and did so with the only weapon she had at her disposal . . . defiance.

As soon as the powder horn was on her shoulder Massy stopped, lifted it in the air and threw it to the ground with such force that her child was aroused from his slumber and began to cry.

Massy pressed John's little body to her bosom, gently kissed his cheek for what she presumed would be the last time and then closed her eyes to await the crashing force of a tomahawk against her skull that would end her life. There was a brief moment of silence, then angry words from behind her. The words Massy did not understand, but she presumed Maumeedoe was cursing.

Hearing the commotion behind him, Alishawa stopped, turned and watched in silence with an amused expression on his face.

No tomahawk blows followed. Instead, the Indian picked up the powder horn and staring angrily at Massy once more placed it on her shoulder. Nothing was said, not even a threat was made. This only encouraged her to once again demonstrate her disregard for her captors. For the second time she ripped the powder horn from her shoulder, and with all the strength she could gather in her free arm, thrust it to the ground again. As she did so she turned and glared first at Maumeedoe and then at Alishawa.

Both Indians were astounded. For until now Massy had not shown her captors this side of her nature. To be truthful, she hadn't shown such contempt to anyone else in her entire life, at least not until now. She was trembling within, but willed not to give the Indians the satisfaction of showing her fright. She wanted her captors to be angry, she wanted to provoke them. And she could tell by the expressions on their faces, particularly Maumeedoe's expression, that she had achieved the desired result. Now Massy bowed her head, prayed for a quick death and waited again.

Both Indians just stared at her in obvious amazement. This was not the docile, meek white woman they thought they had as a captive. Secretly Alishawa was pleased. This woman of spirit intrigued him. He had seen some white women with the British in Detroit who were assertive. But he never had seen a frontier woman of Massy's determination and courage.

Maumeedoe, however, was not amused. Were it not for the presence of Alishawa, he would have done what Massy had intended. He picked up the powder horn and again forced it onto her shoulder. But his resolve was no match for Massy's determination. For a third time she pulled the horn from her shoulder. This time, however, she threw it through the air as hard as she could and all three of them watched it sail over some nearby rocks.

Maumeedoe was beside himself. He uttered a loud verbal protest as he threw his own possessions to the ground and took up the chase for the powder horn. Massy stood still holding her son, but inwardly she was experiencing some satisfaction that she had both confounded and irritated her captors. As he watched his companion retrieve the power horn, Alishawa walked up to Massy, stopped and took her face in his hands. To her amazement, however, he smiled and declared in clear English, "Well done, you did the right thing, you are a good squaw." Looking at his grumbling companion, he added, "He is a lazy son of a bitch. Let him carry his own weaponry."

Massy was stunned. Her act of defiance was designed to exhaust the Indian's patience and bring about the swift punishment of death by tomahawk. But it only served to frustrate one of them and confirm the other's conviction that he had made a good choice in claiming her as his own.

She was not reassured. In fact, she was totally bewildered. Even the death she had been willing to surrender to was not an option now, nor was escape. She seemed trapped in her captivity. And what of her son John, Massy now asked herself, and her unborn child? The one-year-old could hardly retain any memories of home and family. If he lived, he and the next child undoubtedly would grow into wild barbarians just like their captors and thrive on murder and pillaging.

Alishawa enjoyed seeing Maumeedoe irritated. But he knew him well enough to know he had to be concerned about Massy's safety and so he had to become more protective of her. When his growling companion returned with his powder horn intact, Alishawa directed him to take the lead while he walked behind Massy.

So Maumeedoe walked up front . . . and he was carrying his own powder horn. It was obvious to Massy that after the unprovoked attack on her son back on the island, Alishawa didn't trust his companion behind him where he might suddenly do the same to her.

They resumed their journey in the gathering darkness of dusk. Massy continued to be uncomfortably aware of the chill in the air and her aching body. But now she had another concern. Her infant, who up to now had been comfortably quiet, was reacting to the cold. She could feel his little form shivering, so she pulled her cloak about him to retain as much of her body heat as possible. With the Indians preoccupied with the trail they were traveling, she also was able to expose a breast and begin nursing John in the hope of keeping him still.

Evening had arrived when they came upon another forest waterway. It was Conequenessing Creek. From her husband's previous descriptions of the land north of the Allegheny, Massy recognized it. She knew for certain now that they were no longer traveling eastward, but in a northerly direction.

Soon after, they arrived at a location the pioneers called Salt Lick. Massy did not know the name of it, but by her own calculations she suspected they were somewhere in an area referred to by the settlers as Butler. As she looked about, however, she realized to her amazement they were in an unoccupied Indian camp. It consisted of stakes driven into the ground at an angle and covered with chestnut bark. By Massy's calculation it was large enough to accommodate 50 warriors.

This was information that Massy knew her husband and the other spies would find most useful. But she wondered if she would ever have an opportunity to convey that.

She took note that there were several large well-traveled paths heading off in various directions, indicating that it was an encampment that had been in use for some time. There was little time for any other observations, however, for now night was upon them. The Indians ordered Massy to move and led her and her son away from the camp for what she estimated was a distance of several hundred yards. They were following one of the paths up a gulch into a flat, treeless location. There the Indians made camp by cutting away the brush in the thicket. Alishawa then produced a blanket from among the items taken from the Harbison cabin. To Massy's surprise he laid it out on the ground before her and told her to sit there with the child.

As crude as these conditions were, the opportunity to at last get off her feet was a great relief for Massy. The long, wearying trek and the absence of any nourishment had drained her of all of her strength. As soon as she sat on the ground she felt the throbbing pain in her weary legs, the ache across her shoulders and back from carrying a year-old child all day and the painful reminders from all over her body of the buffeting and thrashing she had endured at the hands of her captors.

Her feet were of even greater concern. For now she had the opportunity to examine them and see the thorns and briars piercing through the skin. She had been aware of the pain throughout the day, but seeing them now and realizing the severity of the punctures made the pain seem that much more acute.

Meager as the comforts of camp were, they were appreciated by this weary captive. But not for long. Alishawa approached and without any comment knelt down behind her, pinned back her arms and tied them. He left her sufficient freedom of movement so she could care for her child, but could accomplish little else. Massy's demonstration of defiance with the powder horn had amused him, but he also became convinced that his captive was capable of surprising courage. He wanted to discourage any thoughts of escape.

In spite of her upset stomach, Massy needed food and fresh water after a full day on the trail. But none was offered, and she wasn't at all sure she could swallow it if it was available. The growling noises from her empty stomach persisted nevertheless and she knew her captors were aware of them. In fact, as she lay back in near exhaustion she detected the traces of a smirk on the face of her tormentor, Maumeedoe.

At first Massy was fearful of sleep. She didn't know what to expect from her captors. After a while, however, she realized that being conscious would not discourage either captor if they intended to do her harm. Bound from behind, she was helpless to prevent them from doing whatever their intentions might be. So in this desperate state of mind she held her son in her arms as best she could and surrendered to sleep.

The circumstances were anything but conducive to restful slumber. She was sleeping near two savages on hard ground with only damp clothing to protect her against the night chill. She drifted off almost immediately, and although there were frequent moments of consciousness when she turned her body in search of a comfortable sleeping position, she could not remain awake for long.

But it was not a restful sleep. Massy was not sure what was dream and what was semi-conscious imagining, but in spite of her earlier death wish all of her nighttime thoughts concerned the idea of escape. She saw herself stumbling through the unknown forest with her son John in her grasp and her captors in earnest pursuit.

How preposterous it all seemed. How could she evade the savages long enough to even get away from their camp with an unborn in her womb and a year-old infant in her arms? In all probability, Massy reminded herself, John's cries would alert their captors and thwart any escape. And even if she did manage to get away, they likely would find her. Finally, how would she know what direction to travel? How would she know if the path she was pursuing was bringing her back in the direction of civilization or leading her further into the forest from where she could never survive?

Massy did find encouragement in the Indians' ineptitude. As far as she was concerned, Maumeedoe, despite his physique and size, was mentally inept. His decision to ride a horse down a slippery river bank attested to his lack of judgment about horses. And the fact that the war party had assigned both Indians to guard a pregnant frontier wife, her five-year-old son and an infant was evidence of the lack of respect the other warriors had for the two of them.

***

Once during the night, Massy awoke and discovered that neither of the Indians were asleep. Indeed, they were in conversation.

The conversation was prompted by the fact that neither Alishawa nor Maumeedoe could be certain they were not being followed. Both agreed there were no signs of it during the day. They were aware, however, that because of the woman and child they had not covered as much terrain as they had hoped.

"At dawn," Maumeedoe said, "you stay with the woman and child and I will retrace our steps to see if we have been followed." Alishawa didn't want to trust his companion's ability as a scout, but neither did he want to leave him alone with the woman, at least not yet. So he concurred, but cautioned Maumeedoe to take no unnecessary risks He did not think it possible that rescuers had found their trail. If they followed any trail, he was certain, it would be the main raiding party's trail. But they had to be certain.

Massy was not aware of the subject of the Indians' conversation because they spoke the Miami tongue while they conversed. But by their gestures of pointing back in the direction they had come, she couldn't help but hope there still was a possibility of rescue, however remote. With her arms tied behind her and an infant at her side, Massy nevertheless welcomed the suspicion that the Indians were remaining alert to the possibility of pursuit.

These hopeful thoughts were further confirmed on the morning of May 23 when Massy awoke to see Maumeedoe preparing to leave camp alone. He left quietly, leaving her and her son in the company of Alishawa, who still appeared to be asleep. She also noted that he left in the direction they had come the day before.

"What could they possibly be looking for," Massy asked herself, "if it wasn't the possibility that they were being pursued?"

John awoke hungry and cranky. Massy had no option but to risk modesty in the presence of her captor and nourish her child. So she turned her back, loosened the top of her flimsy garment and brought the child to her breast. She was thankful Alishawa, who was now awake, ignored her. Massy's sense of modesty had always made her seek privacy when she was breastfeeding her children. This prevailed even when she was alone in the cabin with her husband. Alishawa recognized this shyness, so he remained to the rear of her out of respect for her privacy. This did not relieve Massy of her discomfort to nurse in the presence of a strange man, but she proceeded nevertheless.

It was while her child was nursing that Massy realized that the bonds they used to secure her for the night were loose. She had greater maneuverability than when Alishawa bound her the night before, but her captors surprisingly had not even bothered to inspect them in the morning.

"Obviously they are careless," she concluded. It was something she never would have expected.

At last the child had his fill and went to sleep again.

***

Alishawa stood silently across from the captives later in the morning and wondered how many months Massy had been with child. From the size of her stomach he guessed it had been several months. He also wondered if her offspring would be another boy. He could tolerate that in his lodge, even if he wasn't the father, but he would not welcome another girl. She would have to give that child away to another squaw.

Maumeedoe returned to the camp around noontime.

"No white man follows," he assured Alishawa. "I went as far as the river crossing [Conequenessing Creek] and there are no signs of pursuit." Then he grunted. "I don't think they had enough soldiers to send after us or to defend the blockhouse. We never should have left without attacking it and burning it."

Alishawa had listened to this in silence, then he commented.

"Maumeedoe, the blockhouse could not have been taken once we lost the element of surprise. There were only thirty-two of us," he reminded his companion. "With the field of fire they had created by clearing the surrounding land, ten men could defend that fortress for a long time."

Maumeedoe didn't agree, but he wasn't interested in arguing about it.

"The place where we are to meet the other warriors cannot be very far north from here," Alishawa said, changing the subject. "I will scout that trail this afternoon while you stay here with the woman and child."

He deliberately paused to make certain he had Maumeedoe's attention. "Do not harm the woman or the child in my absence. She is mine. I intend to take her back to the village to make her my squaw."

Maumeedoe smiled. It was a rarity for him. "Can't I even have some enjoyment with her while you are gone?" he asked.

Alishawa didn't see the humor in it. "Can't you see the woman is going to have a child?" he muttered. "You already have done enough to her, killing her two sons. Now leave her alone."

Maumeedoe looked away for a brief moment. Then turning back to Alishawa, he concluded, "She will not be harmed."

When the sun was directly overhead Alishawa picked up his musket and walked out of camp in a direction opposite the trail Maumeedoe had used in the morning. Massy was alarmed, for suddenly she was alone with this Indian butcher.

Maumeedoe walked to the edge of the camp with Alishawa when he left and stood there for several minutes after his departure. Then he abruptly walked back into close proximity with Massy and her son. Sitting down before her he glared directly at her and then produced Robert's scalp. Massy was both pained by the sight of Robert's hair and revolted by this Indian's bloody contempt for human feelings. Meanwhile Maumeedoe made a hoop and then stretched the scalp upon it. She could tell he was interested in her reaction, but she was determined not to satisfy his curiosity. In order to keep self control Massy decided she would concentrate on thoughts of revenge.

Maumeedoe was busying himself with this task when Massy noticed that his tomahawk hung loosely from his belt on the ground. She was surprised by his carelessness, for the weapon was not far out of her reach.

"Should I reach for it?" she wondered. To see if that was possible she slowly moved her hand across her knee and nearer the weapon. Maumeedoe did not react. He was still concentrating on the scalp.

"If I could only get the tomahawk in my hand," she thought, "I might be swift enough to bring it down across his scalp with all of my strength."

The Indian still was concentrating on the scalp when Massy put her hand on the handle of the weapon. That startled Maumeedoe and he immediately turned away, pulling the weapon out of her reach. At the same time he cursed her (or from his tone of voice she thought it was a curse) in his native tongue. Finally he remembered the one English word he knew as an expression of how much he despised the settlers, "Yankee," he snarled.

"I only wanted to show it to my son," she explained. "He has taken an interest in your things." Maumeedoe, of course, didn't understand the words, but he knew she was creating some sort of alibi.

It had been a foolish attempt, Massy realized, but she was grateful that he did not extract a punishment for her effort.

Alishawa returned late in the afternoon. He had found no one, he told Maumeedoe, but he wasn't sure what that meant.

"I know," sneered Maumeedoe. "I am certain they found some more forts and settlers' homes and are still raiding."

"Perhaps," said Alishawa, "but that might not be wise. Word of our raid will soon be about the entire territory, if it isn't already, and the white soldiers may lay a trap for them or perhaps they already have."

Maumeedoe wasn't convinced. Neither was Alishawa, for that matter. But he wanted to get out of western Pennsylvania and return to their Miami village as soon as possible.

***

As evening darkened the forest, Alishawa was in a talkative mood. So he came over to Massy and sat down beside her. He started questioning her about the settlers and about the strength of the armies they would be facing. Massy could have answered some of his questions, but she pleaded ignorance. She was grateful the Indian was unaware of her husband's role with the army as a spy.

After awhile he stopped the questioning and began to boast about his tribe's strength. He had participated in the defeat of General Arthur St. Clair's army in Ohio in 1791 and was boasting of his role in the massacre.

"I killed many white soldiers," he assured her.

"What would be his reaction," Massy wondered, "if he knew my husband was wounded in that battle, but survived?"

After awhile the Indian fell silent and brought out the plunder he and his companion had brought with them from the Harbison cabin. As he spread the familiar items before him he picked up Massy's pocketbook and spilled out the contents. They included ten dollars in silver and a half guinea in gold.

Money had never seemed less important to Massy in all of her life.

She did take note, however, of some of the clothing items he had taken, specifically a fresh petticoat and some of the child's clothing.

"What would he want with that?" Massy asked herself.

As night closed in Alishawa produced dry venison and offered Massy a piece about the size of an egg. She was unable to chew because her mouth was still swollen and sore from the blows she had suffered, so she broke the food into small pieces and fed it to the infant.

***

While they had seen no evidence of settlers since they left the Harbison cabin, both Alishawa and Maumeedoe agreed to move the camp to another location within the campsite. They waited until the cover of near darkness then walked Massy and her child to the new site.

In the event they had been seen, they wanted to be somewhere else after dark. Once in the new campsite Alishawa spread the same blanket on the ground for Massy and her son, and once more she was secured from behind. As soon as his attention was diverted elsewhere, however, Massy tested the bonds and found them to be no more binding than they had been the previous night.

It was knowledge she would find to be most useful the following day.

This night's rest proved to be far superior to the first night, even though the ground they slept on was no softer. To begin with, Massy's cloak had dried during the day and proved to be warm protection against the night air. From her first night's experience she also felt confident that no harm would come to her while she and John slept.

But once asleep her dreams were the same as those of the night before. She dreamed of escape, of flight through the forest, of being caught and punished, of not being caught.

5
Escape

A flock of mocking birds and robins heralded the coming dawn as night began to fade the following morning (May 24), waking Massy and her son. The birds seemed to hover overhead and Massy was aware of the irony of beautiful birds singing a good morning to her and her son when they were in such dire circumstances.

She shifted her weight on the blanket in the hopeless search for a comfortable spot on which to lie as she looked up at the singing birds and wondered if they were mocking her instead of singing a joyous greeting.

If Alishawa and Maumeedoe heard the chirping they ignored it and continued to sleep, for neither one of them stirred. So Massy decided it was an appropriate time to feed her child. Turning away as best she could with her arms still bound, she brought the drowsy infant to her breast. She was not at all sure how much nourishment the child was receiving, but she welcomed the calming effect it had on the infant .

It wasn't long before John was slumbering again, along with the two Indians, leaving Massy alone with her thoughts. After two nights of dreaming about escape, the subject would not depart her imagination. Massy even fantasized that the serenading birds, instead of mocking her, were encouraging her to rise, take her baby in her arms and flee into the woods.

"How preposterous," she chastised herself. "I am still bound and in all probability my slightest movement would create enough of a stir to rouse them." True enough, but the thought of escape was persistent and would not depart.

The idea of escape had not occurred to Massy since she and her sons were first taken captive in their cabin. But by now she suspected these supposedly crafty, woods-smart redmen were not as gifted as she first thought. She had seen evidence of one's careless miscalculation in riding a horse down a steep slope and they both used poor judgment in thinking the horses would ford the Allegheny River without being forced by a rider to do so.

Was it possible, Massy asked herself, they would make the greater mistake of presenting her an opportunity to get away?

To escape she would have to be free of her bonds, so Massy tested them by straining her arms against them. She was more than a little joyful to discover they had loosened in the night. In fact, if she had been alone she didn't doubt for a moment that she could very easily slip out of them.

However slight the chances of escape were, these thoughts persisted and gave Massy the first shred of hope since her capture. But she knew that to succeed in getting away the two Indians would have to be separated. She might be able to outmaneuver one, but not two.

While Massy entertained these thoughts she remained motionless and kept her eyes closed. In the event the Indians did awake, she determined that it would be to her benefit if they thought she was still asleep.

From years of listening to her husband's conversation about traveling in the western Pennsylvania territory, Massy knew that if she managed to escape it would be essential to find the Allegheny River. That waterway led directly to the settlements. She also was aware that she would have to travel south from the present encampment to find the river because they had been traveling in a northerly direction ever since they crossed the Allegheny.

"But if I should escape," she was forced to ask herself, "how could I possibly find my way through this unfamiliar forest and get back to civilization?" "Once the Indians discover their mistake," she argued with herself, "won't they quickly overtake me and John and probably end our lives at that very moment?"

Massy reminded herself it would be unwise to ignore the risks if she took this chance to escape, not the least of which would be the one-year-old infant in her arms and a six-month-developed unborn in her womb. Would not these two factors make travel through an unknown wilderness just about impossible?

She couldn't believe the next thought that came to her, for it revealed the depth of her desperation. "So what if they catch me and kill me?" she asked herself. "Wouldn't that be a preferred fate to the ugly future that lies ahead if my baby and I survive this journey and are compelled to live the rest of our lives among savages? We would be forced to become like them and never again could I expect to see the civilized world."

Finally it was dawn and the Indians were up and about. Massy continued her pretense of sleeping and used this time to observe their movements. When she saw Alishawa assemble his weapons and prepare to leave camp she assumed that her dreaming had been for naught and that soon they would be back on the trail. But she was surprised to see his sleepy-eyed companion continue to recline where he had slept the night through.

***

Alishawa had determined the night before that he would search in a more northerly direction than he had the previous day in hopes of catching sight of the main body of Miami tribesmen. He told Maumeedoe to wait at the camp for his return, but assured him that he would be back no later than mid-morning. It was an assignment the younger warrior did not resent, for he welcomed a few more hours of sleep after all of the traveling in recent days.

In truth, Alishawa was anxious to join the rest of the raiding party because he wasn't comfortable on a journey with only one other Indian through territory so frequented by white settlers. He was particularly concerned that his traveling companion was the unpredictable and often irrational Maumeedoe. The sooner he was surrounded by more of his tribesmen the more relaxed he would be.

So at the first sign of daylight he nodded to Maumeedoe and strode out of camp.

***

Massy took note of Alishawa's route of departure. If she could manage to get away, she certainly didn't want to go in the same direction. She was not happy to be alone once more with the murdering savage who remained behind. But with only one Indian present, and he being the more careless of the two, Massy realized she would have to be alert to the first opportunity to get away and do it without hesitation. She knew in all likelihood there might never be another chance.

Maumeedoe seemed to take little notice of his companion's departure. He got comfortable again on his blanket and appeared to fall asleep almost immediately. But was this only pretense? Massy wondered. Was he only creating the appearance of slumber so he could observe Massy's movements as she had done while pretending to sleep? Therefore Massy remained still.

"But how long can I do this?" she asked herself. "Surely he won't sleep all day." She had to test him to see if he really was asleep, but how? She remembered as a child that the only time she could be certain her father was asleep was when he snored. It was worth trying, she decided. So Massy deliberately started to make soft snoring noises as if she herself had fallen fast asleep.

Some time passed before she decided to risk glancing in the Indian's direction. Opening one eye just slightly she could hardly contain her joy when she discovered this was no pretense. Maumeedoe was in a deep, comfortable sleep.

"It must be now," Massy told herself.

Gently tugging at the bonds the Indians had used to restrict her freedom during the night, she quietly slipped out of them and managed to do so without waking her son. His silence was essential, for any sound from John would likely awaken the Indian and the chance to flee would be gone.

Massy had not thought her plan through. Once free of the bonds her first thought was to find a heavy instrument of some kind and bring it down across her captor's head. If it didn't kill him, it would at least leave him unconscious and unable to follow her. But clubbing this butcher was just too risky, she told herself. It would require her to place John on the ground, which might awaken him and bring a tearful protest. If there were no cries from her infant, there still was at least fifteen feet between Massy and the Indian. It was far too much distance to traverse without waking him. Finally, she could see nothing that would serve as a useful bludgeon.

She would just have to get on her feet, take John in her arms and walk out of camp. "Not so easy to do," she told herself, "but what else is left?"

The next decision was in what direction she should travel. She already had decided it would not be the northerly direction that Alishawa took when he left camp, for their paths might cross as he returned. The Indians, she knew, would expect her to head directly south to the Allegheny, so their search probably would follow that route. Massy was seeking a third alternative.

As she looked about at the surrounding forestry she saw a path that appeared to go off in yet another direction. She desperately hoped that would not lead her away from the Allegheny River. But her first concern was escape. If the original course she chose was in the wrong direction, she would at some point have to change and travel south to reach the river. That was also the direction the birds seemed to be following in their flight. So now Massy chose to interpret the birds' presence as a positive sign.

The route she chose headed off into the brush and Massy was afraid the swishing of the bushes and branches against her clothing could create noise. She would just have to be careful to avoid as much contact as possible, at least until she was out of sight of the camp. "If indeed I ever get that far," she told herself.

But for now it was time to make her break for freedom.

Not far from her head was the featherbed case from her cabin which the Indians used to carry away some of the plunder. She had seen its contents the previous day when the Indians were examining it and knew there were some dry clothes that would be needed. And the featherbed case was within her reach.

Taking another quick glance at her sleeping captor, seeing that he still was asleep, she carefully stretched out her hand, reached into the case and felt around until she found one of her petticoats, a handkerchief and a child's frock. Massy's hand was trembling as she extracted the garments from the casing. When she had done so she again looked back at the slumbering Maumeedoe. He had not stirred, so Massy carefully stuffed the clothing into an inside pocket of her coat.

It was now time to take her leave. She could waste no more precious moments thinking about escape. She also was aware that every move had to be made cautiously. And, of course, John had to sleep through the entire escapade.

Massy sat up while holding the infant firmly but gently in her grip. Her hands were trembling. Slowly she slid her left leg beneath her torso and raised her body to one knee. From this angle she could see her slumbering captor out of the corner of her right eye. He still was fast asleep.

Massy wondered why the noisy beat of her heart did not disturb him, for it seemed to beat so loud and clear in her own ears. Taking one more glance at her captor, she slowly rose to her feet.

The sun had been up only a short while, sending shafts of light through the tree tops. "If I can make it out of camp," she mused, "there should be sufficient light to maneuver through the woods.

Now Massy started stepping away, carefully pausing after each step before beginning the next and searching the floor of the forest before each step. Once into the brush at the edge of camp she knew she would be out of sight, but getting there was the hard part.

"The slightest noise can wake him," Massy reminded herself quietly. She looked down at the infant and was grateful he still had his eyes closed.

Massy had to resist the temptation to step away at a faster pace, or even run, for she knew she had to be deliberate. The brush at the edge of the camp was ever so near now and coming closer with each step.

There was a fluttering sound. "What was that noise?" Massy wondered in agony. She heard the sound again. It was from above her.

"Oh my God," she whispered. "It's the birds. They have come back. They will wake him up."

She was only a step or two from the edge of the camp. But she was frozen in fright. Slowly turning her head, she looked back again at the sleeping Indian. The birds had not yet awakened him.

"Get out of here and get out now," she chastised herself. "No more looking back at that Indian. You cannot afford to lose any more time."

Massy took one more step. She could reach out now and touch the tree behind which was freedom. Raising her foot, she felt the child stir in her arms. Looking down she almost gasped to see that John was awake and staring back at her. He was wide-eyed and smiling. "Please God," she silently prayed, "keep the child silent."

She put a finger to her lips as a gesture of silence, but he opened his mouth, so she quickly pressed the finger to his lips. As she did so she took the final step and was out of sight of the camp.

Carefully Massy stepped through the underbrush. She was uncertain about how far to travel before turning south. She knew it was necessary to confuse her pursuers as much as time would permit.

"But how long is that?" Massy asked herself. "How long until Maumeedoe awakens? How long before Alishawa returns to camp and finds me gone?"

Massy knew they eventually would pick up her trail regardless of which direction she followed. She had to find a route that was not so easily detected by the Indians. "Maybe it will confuse them and send them in different directions."

Only a few hundred feet from the camp Massy discovered a scattering of rocks off to her left that led to the base of a rocky hillside. From her husband she had learned that traveling over the hard surface of rocks, while often difficult, would confuse the pursuer about which direction to follow. So she left the path she was following and walked across the rocks. As soon as she did so, however, she was painfully reminded of the deteriorating condition of her bare feet against the hard and sometimes jagged surfaces. But it was an agony she would have to endure, and at least she could be grateful that her feet were no longer leaving a bloody trail behind her. So Massy stayed the course to the base of the hill. Then using her one free hand she carefully picked her way up the slope until she reached the top, stepped over the crest of the hill and finally was out of sight of the trail she had been following.

Putting distance between her and her captors was still her primary concern, but Massy knew she had to get herself and John out of their ragged, wet clothes. She had to risk laying her infant on the hard ground while she extracted the clothes from her cloak. John still was awake, but gratefully found the occasion an appropriate time to again look at his mother and smile, all in silence. She slipped out of her cloak, rid herself of the now tattered and damp petticoat she had been wearing and put on the dry petticoat she had taken from the pillow case. Then she removed her infant's clothes and put him in the dry frock she had retrieved from among the items taken from the cabin.

Throwing her cloak around her shoulders and stuffing the clothes she had removed into the inside pocket so as not to leave a trace for the Indians to pick up her trail, Massy resumed her journey. Her heart was still pounding, but now it wasn't all out of fear. There now was some exhilarating expectation of success also pumping through her battered body.

She could not dismiss from her mind the Indians' reputation for being clever woodsmen. Her husband had grudgingly admired their tracking skills, so Massy knew the Indian left behind to guard her would too soon awake to find her gone. These two weren't the brightest of their lot, but Massy was certain they could follow a trail.

It was to her advantage, she believed, that her captors probably expected her to rush into the wilderness without knowing what direction she was headed. But from her husband she had obtained a basic knowledge of the streams and rivers in the Allegheny River area and knew how to read directions on the basis of which side of the trees moss grew and from the path of the sun.

Unfortunately, she had no practical experience in using these guides to find her way, so she had to learn by doing.

Massy followed the course she had chosen until she came to Conequenessing Creek. It was about two miles beyond the point where they had crossed near the end of their first day's journey. She would change direction here, she decided, and head south. Climbing down the bank to the river's edge over rocks, precipices, thorns and briars, Massy once again was reminded of the condition of her battered feet and the collection of sores and aches elsewhere in her body. But this was bearable in this flight for freedom.

The burden of carrying an infant contributed to her difficulties, including the cramping pains she now suffered in her arms from holding her son in one arm while using her free hand to navigate difficult areas. Once at creekside Massy continued to walk along the stream's edge. A short time after midday, however, she stopped to check her path against the direction of the sun and the running of the stream. With some trepidation she realized she had lost her bearings and was not at all sure she was moving in the direction of the Allegheny River.

The day was passing quickly, so Massy was aware she must alter her course immediately before she was compelled to surrender to the inevitability of nightfall and the end of that day's travels.

First she had to satisfy her thirst, for she had had nothing to drink since her capture. As she knelt down at the bank to drink, however, she saw her reflection in the creek's clear waters and was stunned by her appearance. Her hair was in knots and mud-spattered, her face was dirty and her cloak was a shapeless mass of material. After the initial shock, however, she dismissed her appearance as the least of her worries.

"I'm not going to a ball," she told herself.

So Massy proceeded to drink. After several gulps of water from the stream she cupped water in her hand for her son to drink. A shallow area of the creek was just a short distance away, so with John in her arms she made the crossing there.

To stay at the creek's edge once she reached the other side, she knew, was to court disaster. It exposed her to a much wider view from both upstream and downstream, so Massy began to ascend the creek bank. It was not an easy climb under the best of circumstances. With a one-year-old child in one arm and relying on a body that had been abused and deprived of proper rest and nourishment for three days, it was near impossible. But somehow achieving the impossible seemed to be within Massy's reach.

She had no idea how far she had come or how much distance she had put between her and her captors. But it was getting too dark to travel so at the top of the embankment she sat down to rest and await the setting of the sun.

Once off her feet, Massy rubbed her sore muscles to ease the pain, but could not bear to touch her feet. They were just too sore.

* * *

Alishawa had intended to return to the camp by mid-morning. But he had searched for his tribesmen over a wider area than he originally intended, so he didn't arrive back in camp until after midday.

He became alarmed when he was within a few feet of the camp because of the total silence. He expected to at least hear the jabbering of the infant. His alarm turned to disbelief when he saw the empty blanket and Maumeedoe still sound asleep.

"Where are the prisoners?" he shouted, bringing Maumeedoe straight up out of his sleep and reaching for his musket. The slumbering Indian rubbed his eyes to clear them of their sleepy residue and then he saw the cause of Alishawa's irritation. The bonds used to tie Massy lay on the blanket, but there was nothing else.

Alishawa continued, "What have you done with them?"

Maumeedoe replied, "Nothing. They were there on the blanket sleeping the last time I saw them."

"Well they aren't there now," Alishawa shouted back. "Where are they?" he again asked. "Where did you put the bodies?"

Maumeedoe stared back at him before answering, "No harm came to them from me." Then to shift the blame, he added, "It appears you didn't secure her very well last night. Obviously after you left she slipped her ties and left with the child. But she couldn't be very far, so let us pick up her trail."

It was apparent Alishawa didn't believe what he had heard. He started thrashing through the underbrush looking for the murdered bodies of Massy and her son.

"I told you no harm came to them," shouted Maumeedoe, "and the longer we stay around here and argue about it the more distance she will be able to travel with the infant." But Alishawa was having none of it. He continued to search through the surrounding brush looking for freshly turned turf.

"Show me where you buried them," Alishawa demanded again.

"I didn't bury them. They were still alive the last time I saw them. If you insist on looking for dead bodies that aren't here," he warned, "I will leave and search for her myself."

"Stay where you are, Maumeedoe," Alishawa declared as he walked back into camp, but this time he held his musket hip-high and pointed it at his companion. "We will search together. If we don't find them and I find out later that you killed them you can be sure I will make you pay a terrible price."

They broke camp immediately and soon found where Massy left camp. Her footprints told them as much. But when her tracks disappeared near a rocky part of the forest, Alishawa and Maumeedoe decided to rely on their instincts and head in a southerly direction toward the Allegheny River.

It was well beyond midday when they agreed Massy had followed another route. There was no trace of her footprints and the closer they came to the Allegheny River the more concerned Alishawa became about stumbling into white frontiersmen. So they doubled back until they reached Conequenessing Creek, at which point Maumeedoe crossed and followed the river bank and Alishawa conducted his search on the opposite bank.

It was agreed that if one of them came across the white woman's tracks he would fire his musket as a signal and place a marking on a nearby tree indicating which direction he was going. The other would then follow.

There wasn't much daylight left, so both Indians were aware they would soon have to abandon the search and wait for daylight. They were certain, however, that in spite of the delay they would find the escaped captive and her son before they went too far. The Indians were aware that the white frontier women were not wise in the ways of the woods and that in all probability Massy already was lost.

Alishawa's principal concern now was not just finding Massy, but who would be the first to find her and her son. Alishawa feared for Massy's safety should Maumeedoe get there first. Alishawa knew Maumeedoe was livid over the white woman's escape and the embarrassment she had caused him. He just might find the temptation to kill her overwhelming.

***

Finally the evening star made its appearance, so before the sun disappeared Massy determined the direction she would travel when she resumed her flight the following morning.

Still without nourishment and suffering from exposure to the elements, she gathered a pile of leaves and made a bed of them. With her infant in her arms and under her cloak for warmth and in spite of the pain she was enduring, the fleeing frontier woman was too exhausted to remain conscious. Within moments of lying prostrate on this bed of leaves Massy was asleep.

***

At dawn a discouraged Maumeedoe resumed his search. There was no sign of the white woman and it angered him that a pregnant white squaw with a year-old-child in her arms had escaped on his watch. Regardless of Alishawa's wishes, if he came across the trouble-making woman he intended to kill her and the infant instantly.

He was about to give up the search when he discovered Massy's tracks leaving the creek and heading up the steep bank. He fired his musket as agreed, then moved swiftly to resume the search.

Alishawa heard the rifle fire and came across the creek to follow Maumeedoe. He had gone ahead, but the older Indian followed his tracks and saw the same evidence that Maumeedoe was now following in pursuit of the woman and child.

***

Massy was startled to be staring into the morning sun when she next opened her eyes. She didn't know how long she had slept, and that bothered her. What bothered her more was the noise that roused her from sleep. It sounded like musket fire in the vicinity.

Looking up at the sky she welcomed what appeared to be the same flock of birds that roused her from sleep the morning before. They were flying overhead again this morning (May 25) and their chirping, in spite of the persistent danger of discovery, was welcome. She began to experience the feeling of an alliance with the birds and wondered if they were God's answer to her prayers for rescue.

Massy knew it was essential to move right away, so arising, she began to follow the birds' flight path. There was enough sunlight to travel by and the birds seemed to be flying in a southerly direction.

The night's rest had not cured all of the aches and pains, but except for her damaged feet her body bruises seemed more tolerable this morning. She knew now that she had to travel south of Conequenessing Creek to reach the Allegheny River, so she headed off in what she believed was that direction. It had been almost twenty-four hours since she last saw Maumeedoe asleep in the Indian camp. But it still was too soon to relax. Massy knew she had to remain alert and avoid as much as possible the rustling of branches and bushes. She surmised that they surely must have picked up her trail by now. But how far behind her were they? Massy wondered.

Regardless, she knew she couldn't do anything about that. She had one strategy, keep moving, and that she did through the morning and into the afternoon.

Her curiosity kept her wondering about when Maumeedoe discovered her missing. How long did he sleep before he awoke and saw the empty blanket? Or did he sleep soundly until Alishawa returned?

She could only imagine the sharp words that passed between them over her disappearance, and it brought a smile to her lips. Perhaps one of them killed the other, she thought. "Wouldn't that be just grand."

***

Maumeedoe realized that he was closing in on the escaped woman and child, for as he followed her tracks they were becoming fresher. He was confident he would soon overtake her and he smugly patted the tomahawk stuffed in his belt. Killing her and the child would indeed be rewarding.

***

Massy had made it this far without the use of a walking stick. That was deliberate because she feared the stick's penetration of the ground would help mark her trail for the pursuers. But it would have eased her walking considerably if she had something like that to lean on.

Just about dusk she felt the cold pricks of raindrops on her exposed skin. A light rain was beginning to fall. This alarmed her, for rain would soften the ground and create better footprints for her pursuers to follow. It also would complicate the task of keeping warm. For this reason and because of the fatigue she was again experiencing, she told herself it was time to bed down for the night and hope the Indians were not nearby.

Pine trees were dominant in this part of the wilderness, so leaves for a bed were scarce. But Massy went about the difficult task of gathering what she could to form another bed in the forest for herself and her son. Because of the scarcity of leaves in that immediate vicinity, she had to search for them over a wider area.

"Should I chance placing the child on the ground while I wander about looking for more leaves?" she wondered. "I guess it is a chance I will have to take," she added.

It was a chance, however, that she immediately wished she had not taken, for the hard ground was cold and damp and upsetting to the infant. He immediately began to cry in protest.

***

"Yes, I heard it," Maumeedoe told himself. "It was a child's cry and it came from just up ahead of me." He had neither seen nor heard Alishawa since they parted, but he knew he would soon be coming up the trail. That was why he had destroyed some of the tracks Massy had left and went off himself in other directions. He hoped it would delay his companion long enough to give him time to recapture his prey, kill them and dispose of the bodies.

Now his sole concentration was on the white woman. He would have her soon.

***

Massy was trembling when she snatched the child back in her arms and tried to soothe him. She had no idea how close her pursuers might be and if they were close enough to hear the child's cry.

She began nursing him in the hope that it would pacify him. It worked, but Massy was still shaking. "How far had the child's cries carried?" she wondered. With the infant held firmly in her arms, she

73

stood in total silence and listened intently for sounds coming from the forest.

Moments passed. Nothing.

Then there was the distinct crackle of footsteps against the forest's brush-covered floor. They came from the same direction she and John had just traveled and Massy began to panic. Her footprints must have been discovered, she surmised, and the Indians were now in hot pursuit. Hearing the infant's cries would have confirmed their suspicions.

The Indians had to be close, too close. Massy feared she would suddenly see one or both of them emerge from the forest in a snarling rage.

There was no time to flee, for running now would create even more noise for the Indians to pursue and it was getting darker every instant. She also knew it was highly unlikely she could avoid them in the woods if they were close by, surely not with an infant in her arms at nightfall and with nothing but noisy underbrush in whatever path she chose. Her pursuers would be aware of her every move.

With whatever time remained Massy decided her only option was to find a place to hide. She looked about in a desperate search for concealment. There wasn't much to choose from.

Then she saw a large tree nearby that had fallen across a collection of smaller trees. "That has to be it," she told herself.

As she made her way to the fallen tree, trying as best she could to move silently, Massy pleaded with God to provide her safe refuge. When she reached the downed tree trunk she looked about. No one was yet in sight, so she climbed beneath this mass of this forest growth, hid behind the spreading limbs and used some loose forest greenery nearby to cover her sanctuary. Then she closed her eyes and silently prayed for deliverance.

Moments after she climbed under the fallen tree one of the Indians suddenly emerged from the forest and walked directly to the location where Massy only moments before had started to gather leaves for a make-shift bed. It was less than reassuring when she recognized her pursuer as Maumeedoe.

Now she realized too late that in her preoccupation with camouflaging her hiding place she forgot to bring the infant to her breast. One whimper from him would be all Maumeedoe would need to find them. But she could not now risk moving her arms to correct that situation. Any movement, she knew, would be detected. Any sound would be heard. So Massy momentarily closed her eyes and placed her trust in Almighty God.

The Indian looked in every direction. Then he started to stare directly at the place where Massy was hiding.

"My God he has found me," she murmured to herself, and contemplated one last dash out of her nest for freedom. "Perhaps I should just stand up and let him kill me, for I can no longer bear this fear and this pain."

But Maumeedoe didn't move.

"Obviously he has not seen me," the relieved Massy told herself. "Please God make him leave," she prayed.

Maumeedoe was now relying on his sense of hearing to detect the slightest movement. When he put down his rifle he was so close to Massy that she could hear the sound of his wiping stick against the barrel of the weapon.

**

"She was here, is she still here?" Maumeedoe wondered as his eyes searched the forestry about him. It was obvious she had gathered the leaves at his feet, probably to be used to bed down for the night, he assumed. "But where did she go? Perhaps to get more leaves. If so, she will be back. I will wait."

**

Massy's heart was pounding now and she was certain once again that the savage would hear it. He continued to scan the area. He had not found her yet, but he did not give any indication that he was leaving soon.

"Will he decide to stay here all night?" she wondered. "I will be discovered if he does," she told herself, "for in the morning without the cover of nightfall the greenery will be inadequate to cover us."

Massy glanced down at John and was grateful for what she saw. Once under the tree she and her son were out of the rain. That and the warmth of the space beneath the trees was sufficient for him to fall asleep.

**

"Perhaps she won't come back here," Maumeedoe wondered. "Maybe she is just hiding." He again inspected the various scenery around him. "Where would be a good place for her to hide?" he wondered. He saw several locations that would provide suitable cover, but he was not about to inspect each one.

There was a downed tree across the way, but there wouldn't be enough room for a woman and child to squeeze under. Maumeedoe stood there unmoving and in total silence. He was sure they still were in the area and sooner or later he expected the child to give them away.

***

After what seemed like hours (but was less than one half hour) Massy heard at some distance away what sounded like a bell and a cry like that of a night owl. "Was it a signal from Alishawa," Massy wondered, "or from some other Indian in the raiding party who joined them?"

Maumeedoe's expression suddenly changed to one of anger. He glared in the direction the sound came from. Then he suddenly screamed in response to the signal, looked about one more time and stalked off in the direction he had come.

***

His scream startled Massy and John, but the child did not cry out. Massy thanked God for that and the fact that the Indian had departed. She nevertheless had no confidence that there was any permanency to the protection she had found just in time beneath the cluster of fallen trees. "They will return," she told herself, "once Alishawa hears an accounting of Maumeedoe's discovery of the leaves I had gathered."

She was convinced they would be back by daylight or perhaps before. "And I better not be here," she told herself. So she had to depart now even while darkness was engulfing the forest.

***

Maumeedoe consoled himself with the fact that Massy and her child wouldn't be able to get far at this time of night, so he and Alishawa should be able to find her in the morning. He knew that would spoil his desire to dispose of both mother and child, but he supposed he could live with that.

***

After waiting a few minutes Massy climbed from beneath the trees. It was dark now and the forest was almost completely black. She also discovered that she had remained too long in her hideaway and it seemed as though every muscle in her body was cramping. Moving slowly she managed to struggle to her feet. The stiffness of her arms and legs, the aches in her back, her battered and punctured bare feet were protesting every move. But Massy knew her life and the life of her son depended on her leaving that location without delay.

She wrapped her cloak about the child, put one end of it in her teeth and grasped the other end with her hand. This assured her that her grasp was sufficient to hold him while she made her way in the dark. She shoved the discarded clothes she had been carrying since her escape under the tree. It would confirm the Indians' suspicions that she had been there, but it couldn't be helped. Then she used her one free hand to grope her way between the trees in the darkness.

The lack of light and the necessity that she make as little noise as possible made it necessary for Massy to move slowly. She could not be sure how much distance she was putting between herself and the Indians. Nor was she certain that her path was still in the direction of the Allegheny River.

But she had to press forward. After traveling what seemed to her to be more than a mile she was overcome with fatigue. Once again her one arm ached from holding the child and her jaw was sore from clinching one end of her cloak. She found in the dark what seemed to be a large tree and nearly collapsed beneath it. The rain made the night even colder and Massy shuddered as she pressed her back against the trunk of the tree and tried as best she could to shelter the infant against the deteriorating elements. Despite near exhaustion, sleep came to her only intermittently. But her son was comfortable and he soon was fast asleep.

6
Flight in Fear

our days of wandering in the forest without nourishment while her body was abused and exposed to cold and damp weather was taking its toll on Massy. How she could continue under these circumstances filled her mind with doubts. But she knew that if she and her infant were to survive this ordeal, she had to struggle through the pain, the cold and the weariness that threatened to overcome her.

These were her thoughts when she awakened the next morning (May 26). There were no serenading birds this gloomy day as the dark sky barely showed the early traces of light for the coming day.

"How have I survived this long," she wondered, "without as much as a sneeze or a cold? Perhaps they are taking their toll. Maybe all of these aches and pains aren't due to external abuse and I am sicker than I realize."

Massy was fearful that if her own diagnosis was correct she might suddenly reach the end of her endurance and collapse. "Maybe I'm not far from it," she told herself as she struggled to her feet and prepared to continue her weary journey.

Looking down at the slumbering child in her arms, she knew she had to force herself to keep going. This was her last surviving son. "He must live. He must live," Massy repeated.

Massy's greatest concern, however, was not the pain, the dampness, the cold, or the lack of food. Her principal worry was the fear of being overtaken by the two Indians who were pursuing her and what that would mean for her and her son.

As soon as there was enough light in the woods to see her way Massy left her place of rest and with John held snugly in her arms she moved with as much haste as her injured body would allow. She didn't even stop to feed the child, choosing instead to nurse him while they were on the trail.

Massy told herself that Alishawa and Maumeedoe were probably on her trail already. Without pain, such as she had endured, eating their rations and accustomed to life in the wilderness, she felt certain her Indian captors had resumed their search at first light. "They could be very close," she estimated. "Surely they will find my trail from where Maumeedoe almost found me last night."

Nevertheless, the prospect of reaching civilization and escaping her captors created the energy Massy needed to endure her miseries. As she made her way she frequently glanced down at the contented infant in her arms and this seemed to provide another source of determination and energy within her that she didn't know she had.

***

Alishawa and Maumeedoe had met shortly after the latter departed the location where Massy and her child were hiding. When Maumeedoe heard Alishawa's bell ringing he walked in that direction with the expectation of coming back to that location at first light and resuming the search. Maumeedoe was convinced Massy was nearby and that she would be paralyzed by the darkness and compelled to wait until dawn to move.

His anger over losing a woman prisoner in the woods was exceeded only by his embarrassment. It would hardly serve his reputation as a warrior for it to be known that a pregnant woman with a year-old infant escaped from him in the wilderness.

Alishawa also was angry. He had to grudgingly admit that Maumeedoe had not murdered the white woman. The tracks Maumeedoe discovered at the Conequenessing Creek crossing had verified his claim that the woman walked away from the camp.

But it should not have happened. Maumeedoe should not have fallen asleep. Of course, he also had to acknowledge to himself that had he been less caring about the welfare of the captive and her son when he secured her bonds she would not have been able to flee. "So this is what I get for kindness," he told himself.

"I am certain she is nearby," Maumeedoe told him. "I heard the child cry and when I reached the location where I believed she was, there was evidence she had been making a bed of leaves for the night. They were piled beneath a tree."

"But you didn't see her, did you?" was Alishawa's reply.

"No I did not, but how far could she have gone?" responded Maumeedoe. "It was only minutes after I heard the child cry that I arrived there."

They both agreed that Massy would not try to travel at night in the forest and that they should be able to catch up with her the next morning.

"When we do," warned Alishawa, "I will handle her. She deserves to be whipped for leaving, and I will see to that."

Maumeedoe had his doubts.

***

It was late morning when Massy came across the headwaters of Pine Creek and she started looking for an appropriate place to cross the creek. With the sun's path in the sky as her guide, she was traveling what she believed to be a southerly course. Pine Creek's juncture with the Allegheny River was just a few miles above Pittsburgh, but Massy didn't know the name of the creek or its proximity to civilization.

She kept cautioning herself not to become careless and leave tracks in her haste to find the Allegheny River. She could have waded into the stream at the point she discovered the waterway, but took time to search for a shallow area with sizable rocks to step on in the crossing. After a short walk along the bank she saw what she had been looking for and offered a quick thanks to God for providing a way to cross the stream without leaving a trace of her entry.

As she had before at Conequenessing Creek, Massy glanced in both directions before exposing herself and John to the wider view upstream and downstream. She detected no movement, so she stepped off the bank onto the closest rock, steadied herself and then proceeded to the next rock and the next.

Although each step of the way was a reminder of the deteriorating condition of her feet, she was grateful the cold waters seemed to make the pain less severe. When she was about four feet off shore she lifted her cloak as high as she could and waded into the creek.

Massy knew she had to be alert to the danger of losing her footing. A fall presented no physical danger, for the stream wasn't deep. But the splash undoubtedly would create noise. If that wasn't loud enough for her pursuers to hear, surely her infant's screams from a sudden dunking in the cold water would resound through the forest. John had been endowed with a powerful wail.

Massy stepped carefully but steadily through the soft bottom in making this crossing. Once she reached the opposite bank she took care to climb ashore in some high grass that hid her footprints at the water's edge and then she ducked into the cover of the forest greenery.

Having just resumed her journey on the other side of Pine Creek, she discovered a path not far from the creek bank. Even more astounding were the foot imprints of two travelers. They seemed to be headed in the same direction Massy intended to go.

But were they the tracks of white settlers or Indians? She couldn't be sure. Should she dare make an assumption? Massy was unaware of how close she was to the Allegheny River. She was convinced, however, that she was traveling in the direction that would lead her there. Was it worth the risk of falling into hostile hands to follow these footprints? Her experience just a few hours ago when Maumeedoe stood but a few feet from her was still fresh in her mind. By the grace of God she had not been discovered. Would she be tempting fate to assume these tracks were left by white men?

"I will follow them," Massy decided, "but from a safe distance." She knew she had to avoid making any unnecessary sound that could be heard by whomever was in front of her. "At least until I am certain of their identity." If they were Indians she wanted to be far enough behind them not to be seen and to have the option of retracing her steps before they could discover her.

Massy was becoming wise in the ways of walking in the wilderness. She was routinely avoiding twigs on the trail and low bush branches in her path and ducking beneath hanging greenery.

After what seemed to her to be several miles of travel she came upon another stream that flowed into Pine Creek. Massy stopped and surveyed the surroundings. She had no familiarity with these streams and began to wonder if she had strayed from her intended southerly course. Walking a few paces forward, she knelt in the tall brush and then parted it in front of her.

She was on the edge of a clearing. But even more astounding was the evidence that she had come upon a hunter's camp.

For a brief moment Massy was overcome with joy because a fire the campers had been using was still burning. They could not be far away. But caution prevailed and she resisted her first inclination to rush into the camp and seek help. Avoiding risk was now automatic for Massy and it had served her well, so she decided she would continue to observe the camp until the campers returned.

Time passed and no one came. Massy was not feeling reassured. The longer she stayed the less certain she became about who the camp occupants might be. Finally she decided it was not worth the risk to remain in this setting. Off to one side was a hill and Massy chose to ascend it. It led her across a ridge and down to another stream. Massy didn't know it, but the Indians called it Squaw Run.

***

Even had she known, however, she would have had neither the time nor the temperament to appreciate the irony. But the presence of so many waterways had become confusing. Massy started to wonder if she was lost.

She had to stop to get her bearings, but in her condition, leaning against a nearby tree was a welcome change. "I will just stand here for but a moment and catch my breath," she told herself. But it proved to be a short rest.

Massy heard a noise that came from the forest area just in front of her, so she quickly moved behind the tree she was leaning against in order to be out of sight and dropped to her knees. This was temporary cover at best, she knew, for if the disturbance was caused by Indians she would have to leave in another direction and in a hurry. But first she had to learn the cause of the commotion.

Three deer suddenly burst into the clearing and headed in Massy's direction. Their sudden emergence frightened her, for she knew they had to be running from hunters. But who were the hunters and were they far behind? Her cover behind the tree was inadequate if they were Indians. Now she chastised herself for not departing the area as soon as she heard noise because she might not have the opportunity now to get away.

The fleeing deer were looking back in the direction they had come from. There was a flash and the sound of gunfire. It echoed through the wilderness, frightening Massy and upsetting her child, who began to cry. The noise of barking dogs followed the musket shots.

Massy was now frantic as she looked about for better cover. To the rear was a large log. It was her lone option at the moment, so she went to the log as fast as her condition would allow. Sitting down on it and with the infant firmly in her grasp, Massy started to slide one leg over the top of the log with the intent of slipping down behind it. The deer had seen Massy, so they were now headed in another direction, obviously in response to Massy's sudden movements.

She was grateful for that, for she knew the hunters and their dogs would follow the game. But she still had to get out of sight.

Massy wanted to get down on the other side of the log and remain there out of sight until all was quiet in this end of the forest. As she started to step over the log, however, she heard an all too familiar rattling sound. Peering over the edge of the log she found herself staring directly into the hissing head of a king-sized rattlesnake as it was poised to strike. It was atop a whole nest of snakes and obviously in an ugly mood over being disturbed by Massy.

She leaped back out of the serpent's path. For the moment the deer, the hunters and the dogs were secondary. Having almost stepped into an ugly nest of snakes had unnerved her. The need to get as far away as possible was her only thought now.

Two startling experiences, one right after the other, had her heart pounding and her body shaking. She decided it wasn't worth waiting to learn if the hunters were friends or foes. She would push on in her search for the Allegheny River.

Massy fled out of harm's way as fast as her wobbly legs would permit. But the gruesome vision of that collection of slithering rattlesnakes would not leave her as she hastily returned to her previous route and again thanked God for looking after her safety and the safety of her son.

***

Alishawa and Maumeedoe were not near the campsite, but they were close enough to hear the musket shots. It startled them, for they knew their Miami raiding party wouldn't be hunting in the woods and firing off weapons. It had to be white hunters and they had to be close by.

It had been difficult to pick up Massy's trail because the rain during the night washed away much of it. It also was evident, much to their surprise, that somehow Massy had continued her flight during the night. The fresh trails they had expected to find did not exist, as they would have had Massy waited until morning, after the rain stopped, to flee. Alishawa shook his head. This white woman continued to amaze him with her determination, stamina and ability to survive in this hostile environment. She would have made a fine squaw.

But both Indians had the same reaction when they heard the musket shots. If Massy didn't know how close she was to the Allegheny River, Alishawa and Maumeedoe certainly did. And the closer they came to the river, they knew, the greater the likelihood that they would be seen by the settlers. Now that they knew there were white hunters nearby, it was time for these two Miami Indians to abandon the search.

So both men turned on their heels and headed north away from the Allegheny River settlements and away from the struggling, weary Massy Harbison and her infant son.

***

Massy was now certain that she should abandon any thoughts of rescue by white hunters and continue her lonely flight along the creek bank in search of the Allegheny River. She did so until she reached the head waters of Squaw Run.

This stream seemed to be flowing in what Massy judged to be a southerly direction. Hoping this would be the route to take, she decided to follow it. The rain had ceased, but it left a chill in the air and miserable conditions for traveling on foot. With all of her other problems, Massy was now confronted with slippery footing along the creek bank and the very distinguishable tracks she was leaving in the mud for others to follow.

All of the excitement of the morning had temporarily taken her mind off her miseries. Now that she was back on the trail she was again aware of the chill in the air, her wet clothes and those of her son, and her other aches and pains. Even worse, she had been unable to shield her son from the elements during the night and he also was cold and wet. That he was not crying was no comfort to her. In fact, it was alarming.

"Is the child sick?" Massy wondered. "Is his little body no longer able to resist the ill effects of exposure to the cold and insufficient nourishment?" Her own pain and the discomfort in her arms and shoulders from carrying John no longer mattered. Her only concern now was the child's welfare.

If she could only stop and find some dry shelter. "But in the wilderness finding something that is suitable is unlikely," she told herself. "I can't risk lighting a fire, which is what the child and I both need." And even if the danger of discovery was not a concern, Massy asked herself, "Where would I find enough dry wood for a fire in a forest soaked by two days of constant rain?" So she dismissed the thoughts of the discomfort she and her son were enduring and proceeded along the path shivering against the cold, worrying about her son's health and praying.

Something else had changed. In spite of her preoccupation with the need to maintain silence, Massy moaned with almost every painful step along this tortuous path.

Fortunately, her jaws were no longer sore from the blows she suffered on the first day of captivity. As she plodded along the path she found dried grapes hanging within her reach. Massy reached up and plucked a bunch. She gulped down several, ignoring the sour taste, and fed some to her son. It didn't totally satisfy her need for food, nor his, but she knew it would give her some energy. Energy was in short supply now, so even the lack of sweetness in the grapes could be overlooked.

Massy looked at the sky through the umbrella of trees above her and was discouraged to discover another day was coming to a close. In the excitement of the day she had lost track of time. She and John faced another night in the wilderness; another night in the cold; another night of uncertainty about the route she was following and the Indians who were following her. Then it started to rain again.

Massy had begun to believe her escape was successful and that she would make it back to civilization. But doubts persisted because of her own deteriorating condition and the continuing miseries imposed by the inclement weather.

"Will I ever walk out of these woods into freedom?" she asked in a prayerful plea. She had neither seen her Indian captors nor heard them since the previous night. "But how can I be certain they are not still close by?" she wondered. And now the most troubling doubt of all, "How much longer can I and this infant survive without adequate food and shelter?"

Massy was unaware in her dark hour of despair as she made camp and prepared to spend another night in the woods that the large tree she chose as shelter for the night was within a mile of the Allegheny River.

Sitting against the tree, Massy placed John in her lap, covered him as best she could with her rain-soaked cloak and leaned her head back against the tree. She was overwhelmed with fatigue, but she knew the rain, cold and a body racked with pain would again deny her the sleep she so desperately needed.

There was, however, one positive sign, and it cheered her. When she placed her hand against her son's forehead, he had no fever. It was a consolation she welcomed as another sign that God had not forgotten her.

As the night closed in on Massy and John it brought with it increasing cold that sent chills through her body. Her hands and feet and eventually her arms and legs were numb and they trembled in the cold. John also was uncomfortable, for Massy's rain-drenched coat was little protection now against the chill. He continually stirred in her arms and whimpered, and Massy wondered how the child had survived five days of exposure to the elements.

"How much more of this can his little body absorb?" she wondered. "Indeed, how much more can my body endure?" Despite these concerns for her infant's welfare, Massy was grateful when her son at last was too weary to stay awake and he drifted off into a restless sleep.

Throughout the night as she sat there cold, weary and sleepless Massy was fearful that John would awaken and begin to cry, sending signals out to whomever might still be searching for them. All she could do was pray for deliverance, which she earnestly did.

***

It was a subject neither Indian was anxious to discuss, but they couldn't avoid it much longer. They had found a shallow cave to spend the night and agreed that they were far enough north by now to risk a small fire inside the cavern. Its warmth was welcome relief against the cold they had endured.

Alishawa was trying to chew the toughness out of a piece of venison when he finally spoke.

"It will do neither of us any good to tell our brothers that the prisoners escaped. We must tell them something else."

It was true. The escape was an embarrassment for both of them. The white prisoner had walked away from the camp with her infant child while Maumeedoe slept. She was able to do so, however, only because of the ineffectiveness of the bonds Alishawa had applied the previous night.

"What can we tell them," replied Maumeedoe, "that she overwhelmed us and then fled?"

"Of course not," said Alishawa. "I have been thinking. There were white hunters in the woods. We know that because we heard them today. I am sure others also heard or saw them. It shouldn't be hard to convince the tribe that the settlers attacked us in superior numbers and with superior fire power, forcing us to abandon the prisoners in order to save ourselves."

Maumeedoe stared into the fire in silence pondering Alishawa's words. He couldn't think of a better lie.

"I agree," he said.

7
Desperation

W hat has happened?" Massy wondered when she awakened.
"Have they found me and bound me again?"

The near total immobility of her body gave rise to those fears when she opened her eyes early on the morning of her sixth day since her capture. It was a relief to discover that the bonds were imagined and that she and her infant son were still quite alone in the forest.

"Then why am I so immobile?" she asked herself as she tried to sit up, but could not. Her back was like a board. Moving her arms and legs was equally difficult.

"My God," Massy said aloud. "I am paralyzed. I can't move."

She had feared her body would stop functioning because of the abuse she had endured for five days. Now it seemed to have happened. Her general weariness, combined with the cold and damp weather that lasted through the night, appeared to have stiffened her torso and her limbs.

Was the immobility an indication that she had lost all of her energy and was near death? "I have come this far and endured so much. Surely God will not abandon me here." Now Massy was angry and defiant. "I will not surrender," she told herself. She determined that she would force her body to move, to get up, to take her son and continue the search for a way out of the wilderness. She began by flexing her shoulder muscles. The exercise worked. It hurt to do so, but she could move her shoulders. Next she bent her right arm at the elbow, straightened it and flexed it again. Once again the muscles hurt, but she could move the arm. Young John was cradled in her left arm, so Massy slowly shifted the child to the right arm and then went through the same flexing exercise with the other arm.

Now using her left arm for leverage to raise her body off the ground, Massy struggled to get to a sitting position. The stiffness in her back, shoulders and arms combined to make this another painful effort, but she knew she had to endure it to sit up and at last she succeeded.

From a sitting position she could exercise each leg, bending them at the knees and rubbing the thigh muscles to ease the stiffness.

"What day is it?" Massy asked herself. It was May 27, but she had lost count of the days. "How long have I been lost in these woods?"

These were questions for which she had no answers because recent days and events were all running together in her mind. Massy wasn't even certain that it was still the month of May.

She now could bring her knees almost to her chin and back down again. To be sure it was painful, but she could move them, even though the pain pierced all the way to her thighs. But she would not give in. She flexed her leg muscles again and again. At last the stiffness seemed to fade. All of this activity awakened John and he was observing the exercise with curiosity. "Just don't start to cry," Massy pleaded, for she had enough difficulty trying to get to her feet without having to stop to comfort her child.

At last she seemed to have sufficient flexibility, but Massy wondered if she had the strength to stand up. She was afraid to put the infant on the ground for fear that he would cry out. The last time she did that she remembered what near disaster resulted when Maumeedoe soon appeared. "I cannot risk that again," she reminded herself.

Turning her body into the trunk of the tree against which she had slept, Massy gripped it with her free arm and started to rise to her knees. It didn't work and she collapsed back against the tree. She understood now she would need both arms and hands free in order to get up off the ground. This meant there was no choice but to place John on the cold wet ground and risk his immediate cries of protest. It was a risk she just had to take.

Carefully she lifted the infant from her shoulder and kissed his cheek in hopes that this would reassure him. "Please don't cry," she implored as she placed John beside her on the ground. But he responded just as she had hoped he would not with a loud wail of protest when the dampness soaked through his frock and chilled his back.

Massy had to risk this, she knew, if she and John were to walk away from this place. So she ignored his cries and the danger they might be creating, turned her body and placed her hands on each side of the tree trunk behind her. As John's cries seemed to grow louder Massy pulled herself first up to her knees and then to her feet. She staggered immediately and fell against the tree in an effort to remain standing. Her battered feet immediately sent pains up her legs and she could not stifle a protesting moan.

Now muscles in both legs cramped above and below the knees. The pain forced her to slide back to the ground, where Massy decided to wait until the cramps subsided. "Would it help to walk?" she wondered. "Dare I try, or would the effort be too much?"

Meanwhile, John's loud cries seemed to intensify and she pleaded with him to cease. It was more a demand than a plea, and she was startled by the harshness in her voice. Anyone close enough to hear would be led directly to where they were, and that thought frightened her.

She could waste no more time. She had to get up now. Massy raised her knees and flexed the leg muscles again. It didn't hurt as much as before and the cramps subsided. Gripping the tree trunk again with both arms she pulled herself up until she was standing. This time she did not stagger.

Leaning against the tree trunk, she slid down on one knee, reached out to her protesting son with both arms, and lifted him to her bosom. She wanted to wait until they were on the trail before she nursed the baby, but waiting was a luxury she did not now have after his burst of crying. So Massy started nursing him while still standing under the tree. Once again she questioned whether or not he was obtaining any nourishment from this. But whether he was or was not, it was a tranquilizer and his crying ended immediately. In the total silence of the moment Massy listened for the possible sounds of anyone who might be in the vicinity. But her son's gurgling was the only sound she heard. Once again there were no chirping birds present on this chilly late May morning. But most important of all, there were no other sounds from the nearby wilderness.

Stepping out, she still felt stiffness and pain, so she started walking slowly. The pain wasn't the only deterrent. In spite of some sleep during the night, she was near total exhaustion. After awhile, however, the walking seemed to cure the stiffness in her legs and back.

Massy considered picking up a downed tree branch and fashioning it into a walking stick. But most of the branches on the ground were too large and she did not want to lose the time to break one down to size or create the noise that would come from trimming a branch down until it was small enough.

Picking up where she left off the previous night Massy continued to limp along the Squaw Run path. She had not gone far when she came across another path. This was wide, like one created by cattle.

Indians were not cattlemen, Massy knew, so white settlers might be nearby. The discovery lifted her spirits, giving rise to the hope that she at last could be within walking distance of a settler's cabin.

Massy was moving now at a more brisk pace as she followed the path. As she did so she cautioned herself: "Keep your hopes under control. Don't risk another disappointment." But it was difficult.

She remembered that she had become disoriented as to her location in the wilderness the day before by following a path. It was cause for worry. Would this path also lead in the wrong direction, possibly back into the path of her Indian pursuers or into some remote part of the forest from which she and John would never emerge?

When she had traveled what Massy guessed was about a mile she came to a clearing. And there in the middle of it was a cabin. "Indians don't build cabins," Massy joyfully reminded herself in anticipation of walking into a white settler's homestead. Had she the strength to do so she might have run immediately to its entrance. But because she had to move slowly Massy had time to remind herself to approach the dwelling with caution. Despite appearances, she knew it could be occupied by hostiles seeking temporary shelter.

Massy recognized that for once the pain in her body had served a useful purpose in discouraging what might have been a foolish act. So she rested against a tree out of sight of the cabin and examined the immediate surroundings for some signs of life. There were none. So finally Massy ventured forth.

Well before she reached the building she knew it was unoccupied. There was no smoke coming from the chimney, no activity of any kind outside of the building and no noise coming from within. Despair, which had been her constant companion ever since her capture, was once again overwhelming her as she reached the cabin door. It was quite evident the building had been abandoned for some time.

After wandering in the wilderness all of this time, however, shelter of any kind was inviting. Stepping inside, Massy leaned against the wall. The cabin had a musty smell, which was not at all surprising for a building that had not been in use for a long time. The cabin had to be near a river bank, because Massy could hear water slapping against the side of the shore. But she had no idea what waterway it was. "What if I have been walking in circles?" she asked herself. "What if I am back at the edge of the waters of the creek I crossed before?"

Her melancholy was overwhelming as the doubts about rescue that had poisoned her hopes clouded her mind once again.

"It is beyond all hope. Why continue?" she asked. In spite of all of her efforts the past several days, she seemed always to be arriving too late to find evidence of life. And having not yet found the Allegheny River, Massy started to accept the reality that she probably was lost and with no hope of being rescued. Further weakened by the energy she had just used to reach the cabin, Massy's body was telling her she could go no further.

She thought of just sinking to the floor of the abandoned cabin and waiting for death to come. "What else can I do?" she asked herself. "My energy is spent. I cannot go another step." Death would be a welcome change from the misery she had endured. "It would be an angel of mercy," she thought as she prepared to let her body slide down against the wall of the cabin.

But then she looked down at her son. "What would happen to John?" she had to ask herself. He had survived the ordeal in the wilderness in remarkably good condition. Despite inadequate nourishment, he had been kept reasonably warm and had suffered none of the painful bruises inflicted on his mother first by the Indians and then by the ravages of traveling unprotected through the wilderness. His little body had no cause to be exhausted.

"If I die here," Massy realized, "John will outlive me, probably by several days, and eventually be condemned to die alone in misery and fear with his dead mother motionless beside him." The thought of that fate for her only surviving son after the brutal murders of her older boys was sobering. "I won't quit now," Massy resolved.

Massy knew she would have to return to the trail for her son's sake if not her own and endure even more pain if necessary as long as she was conscious.

***

It was an embarrassing moment for the near empty-handed Alishawa and Maumeedoe that morning when they reached the rendezvous site north of the Ohio River. Some members of the war party had arrived before them and most of them had prisoners or significant plunder to show for their efforts. Two of the prisoners were young women in their teenage years, which was a painful reminder for Alishawa of what for him would never be.

It wasn't long before the other warriors inquired about the absence of Massy and her sons. Alishawa and Maumeedoe shared in the telling of the lie they had earlier agreed to relate in explaining the loss of their prisoners. But Alishawa let Maumeedoe do all the talking when he was asked about the second child's scalp hanging from his belt. He could not understand the pride Maumeedoe showed over the scalping of helpless children.

Neither for that matter could his fellow Miami tribesmen. They soon tired of the details of the bludgeoning of the oldest Harbison boy and drifted away.

When the rest of the raiding party arrived later that day they came with a few more prisoners and several horses taken from the settlers' corrals. Combined with the trinkets, clothes and some household furnishings they had stolen from the homesteaders, it would have made the raid a major success. All of the Miami and Shawnee warriors who participated in the raid, however, knew Chief Little Turtle and the other tribal leaders would consider the mission a failure. They had failed to achieve the principal goal of the raid, which was the capture and destruction of the blockhouse near the Allegheny River just below the Kiskiminetas.

***

Pain and weariness often play tricks on one's senses. Massy knew this. She knew they can make people see and hear things that are not there. Therefore, she dismissed the ringing she heard which sounded like a bell that was off in the distance.

"It has to be my imagination," she concluded. "How could it be anything else?"

But there it was again and again. It was a bell, a cow bell to be sure, and now Massy knew it was not her imagination. She also knew that Indians wouldn't likely be ringing cow bells.

Grateful that she had not yet fallen to the floor of the cabin from which she would be unlikely to rise, Massy struggled to get outside of the abandoned cabin. She started to make her way in the direction of the ringing sound. "Oh, please keep ringing it," she prayed, "and guide me." She assumed it was possibly coming from a nearby settler's cabin, or at least she fervently hoped.

Coming over the crest of a hill, Massy suddenly found herself staring down at a river bank. From the width of the waterway she knew it was not another creek or stream. Indeed, Massy thought this was the most beautiful sight she could ever imagine, for she knew it was the Allegheny River.

Her heart beating at a rapid pace, she called on whatever reserve source of energy she had left in her as she made her way to the river bank and then started to walk in the direction of the bell.

"God bless that cow and the owner who hung that bell around the animal's neck," Massy said aloud, for the bell still was ringing. Only now the ringing was louder than before.

A slight bend in the river bank was just ahead, so Massy took great care where she placed her feet. The surface was slippery. This was no time to fall into the river with an infant in her arms. The Allegheny's banks were known for their treacherous deep areas just off shore. She knew neither she nor John would likely survive a fall into the river in her deteriorated condition.

As she rounded the bend, which was clear of overhanging trees, she was greeted by a glowing light above her. It was the sun, which had been shielded from her during these days by the forest's ceiling of trees and thick foliage. Now it was bringing a bright glow to the morning and an even brighter one to Massy's spirits. So she stopped to look up and enjoy the sight of it in the sky above her.

But Massy's sightline never went that far above the horizon, for instead she found herself staring across the waters of the Allegheny River directly into a fortress on Six Mile Island. She scanned the fortress walls. There was no sign of life. So she started searching the opposite bank

"There, there!" she screamed, as if her infant son could understand. She pointed with her free hand at three men standing on the river bank directly across from her.

And from their attire it was quite obvious that they were frontiersmen.

8
Rescue

Massy was overwhelmed. Only moments before she was in the depths of despair and ready to accept the alternative of death. Now she was standing within shouting distance of her own people.

It was a joyous moment, but because the turn of events was so sudden it also was a shock to her system. She tried to shout the word "Help!" but no sound came forth.

Six days of wandering in the wilderness and speaking only infrequently appeared to have deprived her vocal chords of their vitality.

"Why can't I speak?" she asked herself.

Equally disconcerting was the lack of a reaction from the three men on the opposite shore. When the frontiersmen did not react immediately Massy assumed she had not yet been seen. She shifted John from her right arm to her left, then raised the right arm as high as she could and waved it. At the same time she tried once more to call out but when she started to speak there still was no strength in her voice. Much to her amazement, what came out of her mouth now were only unintelligible guttural sounds.

The men's reluctance to respond was mystifying for she was sure by now they had seen her. Because of the distance separating the two shores she was unable to recognize anyone so that she could call him by name.

Finally, one of the men pointed in her direction. He seemed to be saying something to his companions and now all three were staring at her.

***

"Who is that?" one of the men asked.

"Who? Where?" one replied.

"There on the shore," he answered.

"Oh I see now," said the other. "Who? You mean what?"

***

Massy had forgotten that her appearance was anything but reassuring to these frontiersmen. Her clothes by now were tattered and filthy. Her face, hands and exposed portions of her legs were equally grimy. Her hair, after six days of exposure to wind, rain and dirt in the wilderness, was tangled, matted and unseemly.

She looked anything but the image of a pioneer housewife.

Massy knew she would have to call out to them, and prayed for one last gift from God, the strength of voice and clarity of speech to be understood when she screamed for them to come and assist her.

"HELP!" Massy shouted as strong as her vocal chords would allow. She was grateful that what came out of her mouth was an intelligible word. "HELP, HELP, HELP," she added for emphasis.

At last they seemed to comprehend what she was saying. One of the men cupped his hands about his mouth and shouted the question, "Who are you?"

Massy barely heard it, but she understood they were questioning her identity. Although she did not recognize him because of the distance, the one who called out to her was one of her neighbors, James Closier.

Reassured that she could now speak and be understood, she shouted in response:

"I am Massy Harbison. I was taken prisoner with my children by the Indians in our cabin. I have escaped, but now I desperately need your help."

Massy hoped this would inspire these frontiersmen to finally come to her rescue, but they still seemed reluctant to do so.

***

Across the water the three men continued to talk among themselves. ·

"Can you understand her?" asked Closier of his companions.

The other two shrugged. "She might be an Indian squaw being used to lure us ashore where they can attack. Whatever or whoever she is," he added, "she is in terrible condition." His companions concurred.

***

Frustrated that these frontiersmen were still not responding, Massy cried out again. "Look," she held up her infant son for them to see. "This is my son, John. My other children were murdered by the Indians."

***

Although the men still could not comprehend Massy's message, when she held her son up for them to see, Closier responded.

"She has a child with her. I don't think Indians would risk a child's life to set a trap. I am going after her."

"Maybe, James," replied one of the three, Andrew Burke, "but let's be sure before you stick your neck out."

Turning his attention back to Massy, Burke cupped his hands around his mouth and commanded, "Walk a little further up the shore." Burke wanted Massy to get away from the heavy foliage just beyond the river bank behind her because it just might be hiding a warrior or two. He also wanted to watch the woods behind her as she walked for any sign of movement.

***

Massy understood Burke's command and she suspected that he was in fear that she was an Indian decoy. But when she tried to respond to the command she was unable to do so. Her legs had stiffened while she stood on the river bank and she was finally drained of all of her strength. She was totally helpless. What's more, the pain in her feet had become excruciating. She was uncertain whether she could stand on them any longer, let alone walk. This close to safety, Massy seemed to feel every bruise, every cut and every briar and thorn that penetrated her feet, her legs and her arms.

"I cannot move," she shouted back. "I am too weary. Please help me," she pleaded, and this time the pain in her voice was obvious.

***

Without looking back at his fellow frontiersmen, Closier said, "I'm going over in the canoe, cover me." With that he stepped into one of several bark canoes at the water's edge, dropped his musket in the boat at his feet and shoved off

***

Massy was grateful that at last one of the men was responding. He was paddling the craft in her direction, although even at this distance she could see concern in his expression. His two companions, meanwhile, were taking no chances. They cocked their rifles, brought them up to the shoulder ready position and aimed them in her direction in the event Indians should suddenly emerge from the forest.

Although the weapons were aimed at her, Massy experienced no fear. She was grateful to see the frontiersmen alert and ready to shoot Indians. Indeed, she wished her two captors would walk out of the woods now into a barrage of bullets. However uncharacteristic of her that would have been before she was taken prisoner, Massy now imagined a wounded Maumeedoe toppling over at her feet where she could reach his scalping knife and give him a scalping send-off into eternity.

But there were no Indians. As the canoe drew near her Massy recognized Closier as the boatsman. "James," she called out to him.

But the recognition was not mutual.

"Who are you?" Closier called out as the canoe neared the shore. Now Massy understood their reluctance to come to her assistance. They had understood little if anything that she said. "I am Massy Harbison," she responded, "your neighbor."

But even hearing her repeat her name and seeing her up close didn't help Closier recognize Massy. "I am Massy," she repeated a third time, but he was close enough now that her identity was no longer important. It was enough for Massy that her rescuer seemed to recognize that she was a white woman with a child standing on the Indians' side of the river desperate for his assistance.

At last Closier understood there was no danger and he waved back at his companions, intending that his signal would relieve them of their concerns about an Indian ambush.

He guided the canoe to the shore, then using his paddle turned the vessel sideways and nudged it up to the shoreline. Now Closier reached out to assist Massy and her son into the boat. It was the first time in six days that she felt the reassurance of friendly hands first on her arms and then around her back as she stepped into the canoe. Closier took the child from her while Massy settled in the bottom of the boat, and then handed the infant back as he prepared to shove off from shore.

The return journey back across the waters was under way and Massy knew she and her son were out of harm's way. But she could not speak because a painful lump had swelled in her throat and tears suddenly flooded her eyes. Massy turned and looked back at the fading shore where her perilous journey had ended and where only a short time ago it seemed she was in the last hours of her life.

The shouting back and forth that had taken place had attracted attention in the fort and elsewhere on the island. So by the time the canoe reached the bank of Six Mile Island several inhabitants of the community had come forward, some of them running. With James Closier's tender assistance Massy stood with John in her arms and was helped out of the canoe.

She and her son were safe. They would live. This frightful nightmare was at last behind them. And the flood of emotion coming over her was too much to contain as tears began to spill down her cheeks.

Then the soft, warm, caring hands of women who had come to assist were touching her tenderly. Strong arms lifted her up as someone took John from her and wrapped him in a warm blanket. The soaked, soiled cloak she wore was tossed aside and another blanket was placed around her shoulders.

Massy tried to speak, but the lump in her throat still rendered her speechless. Through the entire six-day ordeal she had not allowed herself the luxury of tears. Other emotions, primarily fear, had control of her. Massy knew she could not afford to break down either in the presence of her hated captors or in her flight for freedom.

But there was no holding back now and the tears came pouring forth. As she was being carried to the fort a stranger put her arms around Massy and rested Massy's head on her shoulder. As she did so the woman stroked Massy's brow with a warm, friendly hand.

Massy's tears now turned to sobs and she buried her head in her benefactor's shoulder. No one minded. In fact, the scene brought tears to the eyes of the other women who were there to comfort her. At the sight of this, several of the men just looked away.

Massy's tears were an emotional mixture of relief over being rescued, a reaction to the physical pain she had endured and the recollection of the abusive treatment she had been subjected to by her captors. But most of all now she wept for the first time in mourning for her two little boys who had been butchered.

She was carried to the Cortus house. Once inside, the heat of a warm cabin and the smell of hot food being prepared were overwhelming. Even though her skin still was cold and clammy, the warmth from the fireplace was penetrating as her rescuers carried her close to the fireside.

It was too much and too sudden. Massy fainted.

While she was unconscious the women removed her soaked and filthy clothing and replaced them with dry, warm clothes. Some of them brought warm water and soap and began to clean her hands and face.

They were unaware that the sudden change in temperature in all probability brought about her collapse into unconsciousness. Fortunately for Massy, Major James McCulley, the commander of the defense forces along the river, arrived from down river shortly after her arrival.

She had regained consciousness when he entered the Cortus cabin, and he ordered her immediately taken back outside. McCulley recognized the symptoms of her physical dilemma and that the sudden change in climate might well bring on shock.

McCulley also discouraged the women from giving her food.

"Buttermilk," he told them, "is all the nourishment she should be allowed to consume at this time." Then he personally took charge of the recovery procedure and spoon-fed the milk to her in small quantities once she was comfortably seated outside of the cabin.

Massy responded and felt her strength beginning to return to her. At this point, two of the women, Sarah Carter and Mary Anne Crosier, took charge of her and began removing the thorns and burrs from her feet and legs.

Felix Nigley, another frontier resident, stood by and counted as the foreign objects were removed. He later pronounced there were 150 thorns in her feet, a figure that was questioned by several of the frontiersmen who didn't believe anyone could sustain such pain, particularly a woman. But there was no doubting the damage done to Massy's feet. The flesh was mangled and pieces of skin were hanging from both feet and from her legs. Some of the thorns in her feet, it was discovered, had penetrated the bottom and protruded through the top surface.

At the sight of her battered feet several who came to assist her wondered if she ever would be able to walk again. That was an overreaction, but Major McCulley told her it would be a full two weeks before she could manage to stand independently on those feet that had walked unprotected through the rugged wilderness for six days.

Meanwhile the infant John Harbison responded well to the care he was given and it was apparent he had survived the ordeal in remarkable condition.

**

Word of Massy's return from captivity spread rapidly throughout the western Pennsylvania community that first evening. The following morning a message reached Reed Station where her husband, John Harbison, was stationed. He was astonished as well as grateful to learn his wife and infant son had somehow managed to escape their Indian captors and make it back alive to civilization. His joy was tempered, however, by the grim news that his oldest son, Robert, had perished.

John Harbison already was aware of the fate suffered by his son Samuel. The child's remains were found in the Harbison cabin after the Indian raiding party departed. Upon learning of Robert's death, a teary-eyed John Harbison vowed to those around him that the death of the Indians responsible would be slow and painful if he ever learned of their identities and whereabouts. And he was reassured by his fellow frontiersmen that he would have their support in seeking this revenge.

**

Massy awoke in a soft, warm bed the following morning (May 28) and was pleased that someone had thoughtfully placed her infant son beside her. It was a joyous reunion.

Major McCulley determined she was fit to travel that day to Pittsburgh in order to relate the experiences of her captivity in a deposition.

So she was placed in a canoe with John in her arms and transported to Pittsburgh to appear before attorney John Wilkins and give a deposition about her experiences.

Even though she had lived in western Pennsylvania for several years, it was the first time Massy had come to Pittsburgh. Sight-seeing, however, was farthest from her mind, so she saw very little on this initial visit to that growing frontier city.

Upon arriving in Pittsburgh she was transferred by coach to Major McCulley's home. There a doctor had been summoned to examine Massy and her son and he prescribed appropriate medical treatment for both.

Men and women alike were astounded when they heard the details of her capture and escape. The weather had been colder and rainier for this late in May. The settlers, particularly the women, were amazed that Massy and her infant son had survived it on their own without benefit of food or shelter.

***

In spite of her poor physical condition Massy was able to give the deposition to Attorney Wilkins in his Pittsburgh office, describing the capture of her and her sons, the murder of her children, the sorrowful trail she was compelled to travel into captivity and finally her escape and ultimate rescue.

***

When John Harbison learned his wife and infant son had been sent to Pittsburgh he was granted leave immediately and set out to join them.

Massy had not been told that her husband had arrived in Pittsburgh. When he entered her room she was in bed and sipping tea. At the sight of his wife John rushed to her side and they embraced. But Massy was unable to speak. She wrapped her arms around his sturdy frame and clung to him with all of the strength she could gather. And she began to sob again. It was a bitter-sweet moment for both of them. But for as long as Massy lived she would never forget that moment when at last she felt John's strong, protective arms around her.

***

Massy's feet and legs were not the only parts of her body requiring recuperation. The exposure to extreme cold, dampness from the rain and then the heat of the sun made almost all of her skin raw. The attending physician informed her and her husband that she would be weeks in recovering and that she would need constant care until the healing process was complete.

The following day Massy, her husband and her infant child moved to a new residence at Coe Station. There Massy gave directions to the Army scouts where they would find the body of her murdered son, Robert. The scouts found the dead boy on the island where Massy said he would be, and they buried his remains there, as requested by both parents.

But John and Massy had to suffer yet another sorrow when the returning scouts informed them there was evidence at the site indicating young Robert had endured more pain than they had assumed before dying. It was their estimate that he lived approximately two days after he was tomahawked and scalped before dying alone and in pain.

***

Relying on Massy's description, Major McCulley organized a force of 150 men to follow the trail the Indians had taken with Massy and her sons. She was assured the Indians would either be brought to justice for the treachery or be brought to a fitting end on the trail if they were found.

But all the soldiers could find was the Indian camp where she and her infant son had spent the first two nights in captivity. There were no Indians in the vicinity. Before departing the scene, however, the men made sure the encampment would not be inhabited again by setting fire to it.

After ten days the force abandoned the search and returned home having found no traces of the marauding Indians and leaving Massy with only the ugly memories of her ordeal.

***

Neither Alishawa nor Maumeedoe ever were seen again by Massy, nor were there reported sightings by western Pennsylvania frontiersmen of any Indians fitting their descriptions. Massy presumed they went back to their village, to more raids on the frontier and to whatever end warriors come to either as young men or as older tribesmen. But their images were forever planted in her memory, particularly the bloody deeds Maumeedoe had committed against her helpless children.

The infrequent considerations shown her by Alishawa when Maumeedoe was his most threatening were not enough to mellow her memory of this captor. In her heart Massy held him as responsible as Maumeedoe.

Contempt was all she could feel for Maumeedoe. Because of her Christian background she managed in time to temper those ill feelings toward Alishawa and the other Indians in the raiding party. But not for this most savage Indian of them all. Massy could think only ugly thoughts about this vicious man.

She knew, however, hate could not fill the painful void in her heart over the deaths of her two children. In time she learned to fold her memories of Robert and Samuel inside a prayerful plea for the end of the frontier wars and the hope that her new American nation would at last enjoy the peace and security of a free country.

Epilogue

I n the fall of 1792, approximately three months after her rescue, Massy gave birth to her fourth child, William Harbison. In the years that followed, another nine children were born to Massy and John Harbison.

Unfortunately for Massy, she never was able to enjoy the tranquillity that life seemed to owe her after her six trying days of captivity and wandering in the wilderness.

The Indian raids on the western Pennsylvania frontier, including the Allegheny River settlements, continued to be a constant cause of terror to the settlers. Peace did not prevail until General Anthony Wayne's victory over the Miami and Shawnee Indian Tribes in western Ohio in the fall of 1795. A peace treaty with these Indian forces followed .

Before General Wayne's successful campaign, however, Massy and the settlers in the frontier communities faced frequent and frightening Indian threats and were often compelled to defend themselves.

On one occasion when the women and children in the settlement were without male protection as Indian raiders approached, Massy organized a flight of women and children by boat before the Indians arrived. On other occasions the women and children fled to the blockhouse for protection. There Massy, whose skill and accuracy in firing a rifle were highly regarded, took her turn at the barricades and helped in the defense of the station. One can only imagine what went through her mind when she found a red warrior in her rifle sights.

In December of 1794 John Harbison moved his family to a cabin he had built at Bull Creek, but he realized the location was too remote and dangerous for his wife and children. The following spring, therefore, the Harbison family moved to Craig Station on Buffalo

Creek. Following General Wayne's victory and the peace treaty that was signed, John Harbison became convinced the danger no longer existed, so in late 1795 the family once again moved to the Bull Creek location.

There they remained for 12 years, but it was not an altogether happy existence for them. The primitive conditions of dirt floors and the lack of a loft in the cabin were a source of discontent to Massy. She also continued to resent her husband's frequent and prolonged absences while he braved the frontier wilderness as an army spy and adventure seeker.

By the year 1817 all of the Harbison children were grown and gone from the homestead, but John's fascination with frontier life was unabated and compelled him to move west. He urged Massy to accompany him, but she refused, so he left her behind and headed for Cincinnati ostensibly to visit one of his married daughters.

John Harbison never returned to his wife and family or western Pennsylvania and in 1820 Massy, who had filed for divorce, was granted it. John died in Ohio in 1822. Massy continued to live among her friends in the Allegheny River settlements and in her declining years she resided in the homes of her children. She died in 1837 at the age of 67 and is buried in Freeport Cemetery near the home where she had been taken prisoner.

The Author

Captive in the Wild is the first novel by Bob McCarthy. Born in 1929, he is a lifelong resident of the Pittsburgh area and a graduate of the University of Pittsburgh. His writing career started during his military service in the Korean War when he served as a US Army war correspondent with the 25th Infantry Division. After the war he was a suburban journalist and editor in the Pittsburgh area for almost a quarter of a century.

In 1977 he was appointed the Chief of Staff to the Chairman of the Allegheny County Board of Commissioners and in 1979 was appointed Deputy Administrator in the Allegheny County Court of Common Pleas.

Today he is a resident of Pittsburgh's east suburbs and is married to the former Shirley Adams. They have three children, Daniel, Laura and Tara.